I0006287

AI 360°

"Explore functionalities, applications, and tools. Leverage Artificial Intelligence to enhance your work, daily life, and creativity, fostering well-being, success, and personal growth."

By Marco Tomasi

Copyright © 2024 by Marco Tomasi

All rights reserved.

No part of this book may be reproduced in any form without written permission from the publisher or the author, except as permitted by copyright law.

2

CHAPTER 1: Introduction to AI 5

CHAPTER 2: Types of Artificial Intelligence 36

CHAPTER 3: Fundamental Machine Learning Algorithms
.... 66

CHAPTER 4: Deep Learning: Advanced Architectures ... 88

CHAPTER 5: Applications of Artificial Intelligence in
Industrial Sectors...................................... 112

CHAPTER 6: AI in Everyday Life................................. 135

CHAPTER 7: Ethical and Social Challenges of AI 148

CHAPTER 8: AI and Creativity 170

CHAPTER 9: Future of AI: Possible Scenarios 181

CHAPTER 10: Conclusions and Preparing for the Future of
AI 194

CHAPTER 1: Introduction to AI

Welcome to "AI 360°", where you will discover its functionalities, applications, and tools, allowing you to understand and leverage AI to improve your work, daily life, and creativity, enhancing well-being, success, and personal growth. This book aims to guide you through the vast and fascinating world of artificial intelligence (AI). The primary goal of this book is to provide a detailed and comprehensible overview of the technologies that are transforming our world, with a focus on both technical aspects and practical applications.

We live in an age where AI has become an integral part of our daily lives, often without us even realizing it. From the algorithm that suggests the next movie to watch on Netflix, to the voice of our virtual assistant giving us directions, to the complex AI systems used to diagnose diseases and predict financial phenomena—AI is everywhere. However, many still do not fully understand what this technology is, how it works, and what its limitations and potential are.

This book is aimed at both those curious about how algorithms and intelligent systems work, and those who wish to gain a deeper understanding of the challenges and opportunities that artificial intelligence offers. Our intention is to make even complex concepts accessible, providing practical examples and concrete references to help the reader contextualize what they are learning.

The rapid development of artificial intelligence has raised a series of questions and concerns, not only technical but also ethical, economic, and social. Understanding AI thoroughly is essential to participate in the public debate and to be prepared for the changes this technology will bring in the near future. Our aim is to provide you with the tools to address these issues with solid and informed knowledge.

Now, let's dive into the heart of the topic, starting with the fundamental question:

WHAT IS ARTIFICIAL INTELLIGENCE?

Artificial intelligence (AI) is an interdisciplinary field focused on developing systems capable of performing tasks that, if done by humans, would require intelligence. However, this general definition hides a wide range of different technologies and approaches, each with unique characteristics and capabilities.

In this section, we will explore the different types of artificial intelligence and how they distinguish themselves. These categories will help us better understand AI's capabilities and delineate the boundaries of what is possible (or not) with current technologies.

1. Weak AI (Narrow AI).

   Weak AI, also known as Narrow AI, is the type of artificial intelligence designed to perform specific tasks. This is the AI we encounter in most practical applications today, such as voice recognition systems (e.g., Siri or Alexa), facial recognition software, and recommendation algorithms from Netflix or Amazon.

The main feature of weak AI is that it has no consciousness or general understanding: it can perform one task very well, but it cannot generalize its knowledge to other contexts. For example, a system that can beat a chess champion (like Deep Blue) would not be able to play another game without being reprogrammed or trained for that specific task.

Practical examples of weak AI:

- Voice assistants like Siri and Alexa

- Autonomous driving systems (such as Tesla's)

- Recommendation algorithms on streaming and e-commerce platforms

2. Strong AI.

Strong AI represents a theoretical concept of artificial intelligence that possesses a deep and general understanding of the world, similar to human intelligence. Strong AI does not yet exist in practice, but the goal is to create machines capable of reasoning, planning, learning, and understanding autonomously, just like a human would.

While weak AI is designed to perform specific tasks, strong AI would be capable of addressing a wide range of problems and situations, with a level of understanding and adaptability similar to that of a human. In theory, strong AI would be able to generalize its experience across many different fields and activities.

As of today, strong AI is still a hypothetical concept, and despite research progress, we are not close to developing true strong AI.

3. General AI (Artificial General Intelligence - AGI)

General AI, or AGI, is a type of intelligence that could solve any intellectual problem that a human being is capable of addressing. AGI lies somewhere between weak AI and strong AI: while weak AI is designed for specific tasks and strong AI represents the utopia of a conscious and sentient machine, AGI is seen as a flexible and adaptable form of intelligence.

An AGI system should be capable of understanding and learning any intellectual task just as a person would. Currently, no AGI systems exist, and their realization represents a significant scientific and philosophical challenge. The debate is open about how long it will take to develop AGI or whether it is even possible.

Hypothetical examples of AGI could include:

o   A system capable of solving complex problems in various fields, such as medicine, engineering, and art, without being limited to a single domain.

o   A robot that autonomously learns new skills, just like a human would through experience and study.

4. Narrow AI (Artificial Narrow Intelligence - ANI)

    Narrow AI is another term that essentially refers to the same concept as weak AI, i.e., an intelligence designed to perform a specific task highly efficiently. The term "narrow AI" is often used to emphasize the limited and non-generalizable nature of the system compared to AGI.

Examples of narrow AI include machines that play chess or Go, systems that analyze medical images to detect diseases, or prediction algorithms used in financial markets.

The various types of AI—weak, strong, general, and narrow—represent different visions of artificial intelligence, each with its peculiarities. While most current applications fall into the category of weak AI, research continues toward the development of increasingly autonomous and intelligent systems, with AGI as the future goal. However, developing strong or general AI remains a distant and complex objective.

HISTORY OF AI: FROM ORIGINS TO RECENT ADVANCEMENTS

To fully understand the current state of artificial intelligence (AI) and envision where it might take us in the future, it is essential to examine its origins and historical development. Today's technology is the result of decades of scientific progress, innovative ideas, and technical challenges that have been overcome. Knowing the past allows us to appreciate the vast evolution that has transformed AI from a speculative theory in the 1950s into a reality that permeates our daily lives. This historical journey also helps us outline future paths, as many of the ethical, technical, and philosophical issues we face today were already raised by AI pioneers. Exploring the history of artificial intelligence is, therefore, not only a journey through time but also a key to understanding the challenges and opportunities that lie ahead.

The Origins: Alan Turing and the "Turing Test"

The history of AI begins in the 1950s with one of the greatest mathematicians and logicians of the 20th century, Alan Turing. Considered the "father of computer science" and one of AI's conceptual founders, Turing laid the groundwork for artificial intelligence theory in 1950 with his famous paper, "Computing Machinery and Intelligence." In this pioneering work, Turing posed a question that would become central to the AI debate: "Can machines think?"

To answer this question, Turing proposed an experiment known as the Turing Test, a method to determine whether a machine can exhibit behavior indistinguishable from that of a human. The test involves three participants: a human who asks questions, another human, and a machine that responds. If the human judge cannot distinguish between the machine's and the human's responses, the machine can be considered "intelligent."

Although the Turing Test sparked numerous philosophical and scientific debates, it remains a milestone in AI development. Not so much for the test itself, but for the idea that a machine could imitate human thought through algorithms and logical processes. This was the first step toward developing a science aimed at replicating or simulating human intelligence.

The 1950s and 1960s: The Birth of AI as a Research Field

Building on Turing's ideas, the 1950s laid the foundation for AI as a scientific research discipline. In 1956, a conference at Dartmouth College was the first official event where the term "artificial intelligence" was used. Researchers John McCarthy, Marvin Minsky, Nathaniel Rochester, and Claude Shannon organized the meeting to explore how to create machines capable of performing tasks requiring human intelligence, such as playing chess, solving mathematical problems, and understanding natural language.

In the following years, the first AI programs were developed. One of the most notable was Logic Theorist, developed by Allen Newell and Herbert A. Simon between 1955 and 1956, which was able to prove mathematical logic theorems, including one more elegant than a proof published by Bertrand Russell and Alfred North Whitehead. This program was considered one of the first practical examples of AI.

Another significant step in this period was the General Problem Solver (GPS), a program that sought to solve problems using a goal-based search strategy. Although it couldn't solve complex problems, it was an ambitious attempt to create a machine capable of addressing a wide range of tasks.

Despite the initial enthusiasm, AI research soon encountered technical limitations, mainly due to the lack of computing power and the difficulty of representing complex knowledge in a way that computers could process.

The 1970s: The AI Winter

In the 1970s, artificial intelligence entered a period of slowdown known as the "AI Winter." This term refers to the decline in interest and funding for AI research, caused by the failure of technologies to live up to earlier promises.

Early AI systems, such as those that attempted to solve mathematical problems or play chess, had shown significant limitations. Although they worked well in narrow domains, they could not handle more complex or general tasks. Moreover, the computing power of the time was insufficient to support researchers' more ambitious ideas. Frustration grew, and many investors and governments reduced funding for AI research.

Despite the AI Winter, some progress continued. During this period, Marvin Minsky and Seymour Papert openly criticized neural networks, hindering the development of this technology for decades. However, advances were made in expert systems, a form of rule-based AI that solved problems in specific domains, such as medical diagnosis.

The 1980s: The Return of AI and Expert Systems

In the 1980s, artificial intelligence experienced a revival thanks to the development of expert systems, software designed to replicate human decision-making processes in a specific field. One of the most notable examples is XCON, an expert system developed by Digital Equipment Corporation (DEC) to configure their computer systems. XCON significantly reduced the time needed to configure computers, demonstrating the commercial value of AI.

This success, combined with increasing computing power and new approaches to machine learning, brought AI back into the spotlight. However, the limitations of these systems soon became apparent: expert systems were difficult to maintain and update, as they required the manual input of rules by human experts.

The 1990s: Neural Networks and Deep Blue's Victory

At the end of the 1980s and the beginning of the 1990s, there was a resurgence of interest in neural networks, an approach that mimicked the structure of the human brain to solve complex problems. The discovery of the backpropagation algorithm allowed for more efficient training of multi-layer neural networks, reigniting interest in this technology.

A symbolic event of the 1990s was IBM's Deep Blue defeating world chess champion Garry Kasparov in 1997. This marked the first time a machine defeated a world chess champion, demonstrating the power of computers in solving complex problems.

The 21st Century: Big Data, Machine Learning, and Deep Learning

The early 21st century marked a significant turning point in the development of artificial intelligence, mainly due to the exponential increase in computing power, data availability, and advances in machine learning. The era of big data and access to vast datasets transformed AI's capabilities, enabling more complex and powerful algorithms. During this period, two key research areas—machine learning and deep learning—emerged as dominant technologies, bringing AI from laboratory experiments to widespread adoption in commercial and industrial sectors.

The Rise of Big Data

In the early 2000s, with the growth of global connectivity and the internet boom, there was a sharp increase in the amount of data generated. Tech companies like Google, Amazon, and Facebook began collecting vast amounts of user data, creating fertile ground for applying machine learning algorithms on a large scale. The term "big data" refers to the analysis of datasets so large and complex that traditional data management techniques cannot handle them.

Big data was a key enabler for AI development, as machine learning algorithms require vast amounts of data to improve their decision-making accuracy. With the growth of social media platforms, e-commerce, and mobile devices, AI began finding applications in a wide range of sectors, from consumer analysis to healthcare, and even targeted advertising.

Machine Learning: A Game-Changer

Machine learning, the ability of machines to learn from data and improve their performance without being explicitly programmed for every task, became the cornerstone of modern AI. In 2006, Geoffrey Hinton, a pioneer in neural networks, introduced the concept of deep learning, a machine learning technique that uses neural networks with many layers to extract hierarchical data representations.

Throughout the 2000s, researchers refined supervised and unsupervised learning algorithms, enabling accurate classification, data clustering, and trend prediction. Some of the most widely used algorithms include:

- Support Vector Machines (SVMs): used to classify data into two categories.

- Random Forests: algorithms that build a "forest" of decision trees to improve prediction accuracy.

- K-means Clustering: an unsupervised learning technique that groups data based on similarities.

Machine learning found applications in industries like marketing, finance, medical diagnosis, and predicting online user behavior. For example, machine learning algorithms were fundamental to developing recommendation systems used by platforms like Netflix and Amazon to suggest movies or products based on user preferences.

The Explosion of Deep Learning

The true turning point for modern artificial intelligence came with the explosion of deep learning in the early 2010s. Thanks to the combination of deep neural networks and powerful GPUs (graphics processing units), deep learning enabled the rapid and accurate processing of enormous amounts of data. Deep neural networks are mathematical models inspired by the structure of the human brain, where data is processed through multiple layers (or "neurons"), allowing the recognition of complex patterns that would be difficult to detect with other algorithms.

One of the first practical demonstrations of deep learning's power was presented in 2012 when AlexNet, a convolutional neural network (CNN) architecture, won the ImageNet Large Scale Visual Recognition Challenge by a significant margin. This result showed that deep neural networks could far surpass traditional approaches in image recognition. From that point, deep learning began being applied in a wide range of sectors:

- Facial recognition: algorithms that recognize faces in real-time, used in security and social media.

- Natural language processing (NLP): chatbots, automatic translators, and voice assistants like Siri and Google Assistant.

- Autonomous driving: self-driving cars use deep neural networks to analyze their surroundings in real-time and make driving decisions.

Convolutional neural networks (CNNs) proved particularly effective for image and video recognition, while recurrent neural networks (RNNs), which retain memory of previous information, have found applications in automatic translation and time-series forecasting.

The Rise of Transformers and Language Models

Another major change in the 2010s was the development of language models based on transformers, which revolutionized the field of natural language processing (NLP). In 2017, a team of Google researchers introduced the Transformer model, which changed how deep learning models process sequences of data.

Unlike recurrent neural networks (RNNs), transformers can process entire sequences of words or phrases simultaneously, making them much more efficient and capable of capturing long-term relationships between words in a text. This innovation led to the development of models like BERT (Bidirectional Encoder Representations from Transformers) and later the GPT (Generative Pre-trained Transformer) family, such as GPT-3, one of the most advanced text generation models in the world.

Developed by OpenAI and launched in 2020, GPT-3 is a model capable of generating natural language texts in a wide range of styles and contexts. Trained on billions of parameters, GPT-3 demonstrated remarkable abilities in generating articles, poetry, computer code, and even convincing conversations. The rise of transformer-based language models has opened the door to new applications, including advanced chatbots, real-time translators, and increasingly sophisticated personal assistants.

DIFFERENCE BETWEEN AI, MACHINE LEARNING, AND DATA SCIENCE

Artificial Intelligence (AI), Machine Learning (ML), and Data Science are terms often used interchangeably, but they represent distinct disciplines that intersect in many areas. Understanding the differences between these fields is essential for anyone who wants to delve deeper into the role these technologies play in digital transformation and innovation.

Artificial Intelligence (AI)

Artificial Intelligence (AI) is the broadest of the three fields and refers to the creation of machines and systems capable of performing tasks that typically require human intelligence, such as problem-solving, reasoning, learning, and understanding language. The goal of AI is to create algorithms and systems that can simulate intelligent behavior.

AI includes subfields such as:

- Natural Language Processing (NLP): for example, voice assistants like Siri and Alexa.

- Image Recognition: for example, facial recognition used in security and social media.

- Intelligent Automation: such as autonomous vehicles.

In short, AI is a broad umbrella that includes various techniques to make a machine "intelligent," many of which rely on machine learning.

Machine Learning (ML)

Machine learning (ML) is a sub-discipline of AI that focuses on algorithms that enable machines to learn from data and improve their performance over time without being explicitly programmed. In other words, instead of programming a machine to perform specific tasks, machine learning systems learn autonomously from data through training.

Practical example of machine learning: Netflix or Amazon recommendation engines that learn from user preferences to suggest new movies or products. Every time you watch a movie or series, the system records details such as genre, duration, actors, and ratings. This data is combined with the behavior of similar users to create a personalized profile. The algorithm automatically learns your preferences, adapts over time, and suggests content you might like. For instance, if you frequently watch thrillers, the system will recommend more films or series in that genre, improving with each interaction— completely autonomously.

Data Science

Data Science is a multidisciplinary field that combines expertise in statistics, programming, and data analysis to extract valuable insights from complex datasets. A data scientist's work involves collecting, cleaning, analyzing, and modeling data, using statistical tools and machine learning algorithms to provide useful insights for business or scientific decisions.

Unlike AI, data science does not necessarily focus on creating intelligent systems. It is concerned with transforming data into actionable information, with the goal of finding patterns, making predictions, or optimizing business processes. However, data science often uses machine learning techniques to analyze data.

Practical example: Predictive sales analysis for a company, where a data scientist uses historical sales data to forecast future trends.

How They Intersect

- AI and Machine Learning: AI is the overarching goal of creating intelligent machines, while machine learning is one of the key techniques used to achieve this goal.

- Machine Learning and Data Science: Data scientists often use machine learning techniques to build predictive models and find hidden patterns in data.

- AI and Data Science: AI can use data science tools to collect and analyze data, but its purpose goes beyond data analysis—it aims to make machines capable of autonomous decision-making.

In summary, artificial intelligence is the general concept, machine learning is one of its fundamental tools, and data science is a discipline that uses ML techniques to analyze data and produce useful information for various industries.

Classical Programming vs. Artificial Intelligence

Another important concept to clarify is the difference between classical programming and artificial intelligence (AI): they differ primarily in how they approach problems and make decisions.

In classical programming, developers write precise, detailed instructions that the machine must execute. Every step is explicitly coded, and the computer follows the rules defined by the programmer. Essentially, the programmer must anticipate every possible scenario and provide a solution for each. This approach works well for deterministic problems, such as mathematical calculations or file management, where predefined answers exist.

The programmer provides the computer with explicit instructions on how to execute each step. A practical example is a calculator. If we wanted to create a program that performs a simple operation like addition, we would write code that follows fixed rules: (a+b=?). In this case, the programmer clearly defines that the program must take two numbers (a and b), add them, and return the result. There is no room for error or learning: the computer does exactly what it was told—add two numbers. If the user inputs something other than numbers, the program will not function correctly unless the programmer explicitly provides a case to handle the error.

This approach works well for simple and predictable problems, where clear instructions can be given for every possible input. However, it becomes less effective when dealing with complex problems that require adaptability or decisions based on uncertain or variable data—something that AI can handle by learning from data.

In contrast, AI takes a more adaptive and flexible approach. Instead of being programmed with fixed rules, AI is "trained" using large amounts of data. AI models, such as those used in machine learning, learn from the data to recognize patterns and make predictions or decisions. In this case, the programmer doesn't write every rule explicitly but creates algorithms capable of learning and improving with experience. For example, a facial recognition algorithm does not have fixed rules on how to recognize a face but learns through thousands of examples.

Therefore, while classical programming is static and follows rigid rules, AI is dynamic and adapts to the data. Classical programming requires explicit instructions for every task, whereas AI learns from data to handle complex and variable tasks.

AI IN USE TODAY

Artificial intelligence (AI) has become an integral part of daily life, often without us even realizing it. From search engines to content recommendations, from chatbots to autonomous vehicles, AI is now omnipresent and plays a crucial role in many of the activities we perform every day. In this section, we will examine some of the most common applications of AI, providing concrete examples and highlighting how these technologies influence our lives.

1. Search Engines

   One of the most common applications of artificial intelligence is in search engines like Google, Bing, and Yahoo. Every time we perform an internet search, machine learning algorithms and AI are used to improve the results. These algorithms analyze vast amounts of data to determine which websites, articles, or pages are most relevant based on the user's search query.

Google, in particular, uses AI to continuously improve its page ranking algorithm, considering factors such as content relevance, the quality of external links, and the behavior of previous users with similar searches. In recent years, Google introduced BERT (Bidirectional Encoder Representations from Transformers), a natural language model based on deep neural networks that better understands the context of complex queries, significantly improving the quality of the responses provided to users.

2. Recommendation Algorithms

Another fundamental application of AI is in recommendation systems, used by streaming platforms like Netflix and Amazon. These recommendation algorithms analyze user behavior and preferences to suggest personalized content, such as movies, TV series, or products to purchase.

For instance, Netflix uses machine learning algorithms to examine a user's viewing history and compare it with others who have similar preferences. By doing so, it can suggest films or series the user might enjoy. The same applies to Amazon, where AI analyzes purchasing habits and product views to recommend relevant items. These recommendation systems are designed to enhance the user experience, optimizing interactions and increasing the likelihood of satisfaction or purchase.

3. Chatbots and Virtual Assistants

In recent years, the use of chatbots and virtual assistants has grown significantly, both in commerce and customer service. Voice assistants like Siri (Apple), Alexa (Amazon), and Google Assistant use AI and natural language processing (NLP) to understand user requests and provide responses or carry out appropriate actions.

These systems leverage machine learning and deep learning techniques to improve their performance over time, learning from past interactions to provide more accurate responses. For example, Alexa can control smart home devices, answer questions, play music, and even place orders on Amazon. Chatbots, on the other hand, are often used by e-commerce companies and banking services to provide automated customer support, answering frequently asked questions or helping resolve common issues in real time.

4. Autonomous Driving

One of the most advanced developments in AI is in the field of autonomous driving. Companies like Tesla, Waymo (a subsidiary of Alphabet/Google), and Uber are developing vehicles that use deep learning algorithms and neural networks to navigate traffic, recognize road signs, detect obstacles, and make autonomous driving decisions.

Autonomous vehicles use a combination of sensors (cameras, lidar, radar) and AI to interpret their surroundings in real time and react safely. These vehicles must make complex decisions in milliseconds, such as stopping at a red light or avoiding a pedestrian, all without human intervention. While autonomous driving technology is not yet fully perfected, the underlying technologies are rapidly advancing, and the industry is expected to continue evolving in the coming years.

5. AI in E-Commerce

In e-commerce, AI is used to enhance the user's shopping experience. In addition to recommendation systems, e-commerce sites use machine learning algorithms to optimize internal search operations and suggest related products. Furthermore, AI is used to analyze user behavioral data, improving marketing strategies and personalized advertising campaigns.

Predictive analytics techniques, based on machine learning, allow retailers to forecast future sales trends and improve inventory management, reducing costs and increasing customer satisfaction. Another interesting aspect is AI-powered visual search, which allows users to search for products by uploading images instead of entering keywords.

Artificial intelligence is already deeply embedded in our daily lives, improving the efficiency and quality of our interactions with technology. From search engines to voice assistants, from recommendation systems to autonomous vehicles, AI is revolutionizing how we live, work, and entertain ourselves. However, this is only the beginning. As AI becomes more advanced, its impact will continue to grow, opening new opportunities in many other sectors.

KEY PLAYERS IN AI TODAY AND THE ROLE OF BIG TECH

In recent years, artificial intelligence (AI) has experienced an unprecedented surge in media coverage and technological advancement. Technologies like OpenAI's ChatGPT and Google Gemini are redefining how we interact with technology, while giants like Apple, Microsoft, Meta, NVIDIA, and prominent figures such as Elon Musk are pushing AI toward new frontiers. At the same time, the growing demand for AI solutions has led many companies to use AI as a marketing tool, sometimes excessively or in ways that may not make sense.

OpenAI and ChatGPT: Generative AI Revolutionizing the Sector

OpenAI has become one of the most influential organizations in the field of artificial intelligence, thanks to language models like ChatGPT. Powered by GPT-3 and GPT-4 models, this tool has demonstrated exceptional capabilities in understanding and generating natural language text, which has had a huge impact across many sectors.

ChatGPT is used in applications like customer service automation, content creation, writing assistance, and software development. Due to its versatility, ChatGPT quickly gained popularity and paved the way for widespread adoption of generative AI models. The use of automatic text generation has changed the way companies interact with customers, develop software, and create marketing content, reducing time and increasing efficiency.

The impact of ChatGPT has been so profound that it has drawn worldwide attention to generative AI, becoming a benchmark for the evolution of artificial intelligence and compelling competitors to respond with their own innovative solutions.

Google Gemini: Google's AI Relaunch

Google, one of the pioneers of AI, responded to the rapid growth of OpenAI with the launch of Google Gemini. Gemini is a suite of AI models aimed at overcoming the limitations of natural language processing (NLP) by introducing multimodal capabilities, meaning the ability to understand text, images, and videos simultaneously.

Google has historically used artificial intelligence to improve its core services, such as the search engine, Gmail, and YouTube, but Gemini represents a new generation of more versatile and advanced AI. Thanks to Gemini, Google is integrating AI across all its platforms, aiming to enhance user experience with more contextual responses and the automation of complex tasks. The company has also integrated this technology into Google Cloud, offering businesses powerful tools for data management and the automation of daily operations.

The launch of Google Gemini has allowed the company to reposition itself as a leader in AI, directly competing with OpenAI and solidifying its position in the artificial intelligence landscape.

Microsoft: OpenAI Ecosystem and the Power of Azure

Microsoft has adopted a clear strategy in artificial intelligence, becoming one of OpenAI's main partners. Its multibillion-dollar investment in OpenAI has led to deep integration of GPT technologies into various Microsoft products, including Microsoft 365 and Azure. The launch of Copilot, a feature that leverages generative AI to automate tasks in Word, Excel, and other tools, has transformed productivity in the business environment.

Azure, Microsoft's cloud platform, has become one of the main infrastructures for training and deploying AI models. Microsoft has made advanced AI tools available to companies, allowing them to develop customized large-scale solutions. The integration of AI into Bing, Microsoft's search engine, has also enhanced search and suggestion capabilities, transforming the way users interact with search results.

Apple: The Quiet but Powerful Approach to AI

Apple has been more discreet than other companies in announcing its AI advancements, but it has certainly not lagged behind in the revolution. The company has integrated AI into its products through technologies like Siri, which uses AI for voice processing, and Face ID, the facial recognition system based on machine learning. However, Apple has distinguished itself by its focus on privacy and data security, implementing AI models that operate directly on devices rather than in the cloud.

Apple has also invested heavily in AI for computational photography, improving image quality on iPhones using advanced machine learning techniques that optimize light management, detail, and color.

Although it has not made headline-grabbing announcements like OpenAI or Google, Apple is working to make AI an invisible yet crucial part of the user experience, with an emphasis on simplicity and privacy.

NVIDIA: The Engine of Modern AI

NVIDIA is undoubtedly one of the major players in the recent AI explosion. While companies like OpenAI and Google develop software, NVIDIA provides the hardware that makes large-scale AI model training and execution possible. Its GPUs (graphics processing units) have become the standard for parallel computing, essential for training deep neural networks.

NVIDIA's growth has been driven by the increasing demand for artificial intelligence and deep learning solutions, as more companies rely on high-performance GPUs to process large volumes of data. Its NVIDIA AI Enterprise software platform provides the necessary tools to develop, train, and deploy AI models, making it a key player not only in gaming and graphics but also in sectors such as healthcare, automotive (contributing to the development of autonomous vehicles), and manufacturing.

The recent surge in NVIDIA's stock reflects the huge demand for its products, driven by AI's evolution. The company is capitalizing on the global need to accelerate technological innovation, becoming one of the world's most valuable companies.

Meta and the Metaverse: Zuckerberg's Vision for AI

Meta (formerly Facebook) has an interesting approach to artificial intelligence, deeply integrating it into its social platforms and the metaverse. Meta's machine learning algorithms are at the heart of managing Facebook and Instagram news feeds, as well as ad recommendations and content moderation.

However, Meta's real bet is on integrating AI into the metaverse, a virtual space where artificial intelligence will play a key role in interaction and content creation. Meta is developing intelligent avatars, models for creating virtual environments, and language automation tools to enhance user experience in the metaverse. Although the metaverse project is still in development, AI will be a fundamental component in realizing this vision.

Elon Musk and the Search for Safe AI

Elon Musk, founder of Tesla and SpaceX, is known for his controversial opinions on AI. Despite being a co-founder of OpenAI, Musk has expressed concerns about the safety of advanced artificial intelligence, fearing that uncontrolled AI development could pose an existential risk to humanity.

Tesla, under Musk's leadership, is heavily using AI in the development of its autonomous vehicles, with deep learning systems that enable cars to make real-time decisions. Musk is also working on Neuralink, a brain-computer interface project aimed at merging human intelligence with AI.

AI as a Marketing Tool: Success or Excess?

The enormous media impact of artificial intelligence has led many companies to include AI in every marketing campaign. In many cases, the use of AI truly improves products or services. However, the growing media pressure has caused many companies to use the term "AI" even when its application is marginal or not particularly innovative.

In various sectors, we see AI adoption more as a branding strategy than true innovation, with companies promoting "AI-based products" that, in reality, are basic automations. This excessive use of the term risks confusing consumers and undermining trust in AI as a transformative technology.

FUTURE PERSPECTIVES ON AI: GENERAL AI, SUPERINTELLIGENCE, AND THE IMPACT OF QUANTUM COMPUTERS

Artificial intelligence has already demonstrated its revolutionary potential, transforming industries, daily habits, and human interactions. However, what we have seen so far is only the beginning of what AI could achieve. With the rapid advancement of technologies such as general AI and superintelligence, the future of AI looks even more radical and complex. In this section, we will analyze the possible directions in which AI development is heading, such as achieving Artificial General Intelligence (AGI) and the emergence of superintelligence, concepts that will be explored in greater depth in subsequent chapters.

General AI: Toward Versatile and Adaptable Intelligence

To date, most applications of artificial intelligence are based on narrow or specific AI, designed to solve limited and specialized problems. These systems, such as ChatGPT or image recognition models, excel at specific tasks but lack a general understanding of the world. For example, while an AI can beat the world chess champion, it cannot automatically apply the same intelligence to other games or tasks without being reprogrammed or retrained.

The ultimate goal of many researchers is to create Artificial General Intelligence (AGI), a machine capable of performing any intellectual task that a human could accomplish. AGI would be able to learn, adapt, and improve on any subject or problem, regardless of context. It would be a machine with a broad and flexible understanding, capable of reasoning through unforeseen problems or tasks not specifically programmed.

While the development of AGI still seems distant, recent breakthroughs in machine learning, neural networks, and natural language processing suggest that we are making significant progress in this direction. However, AGI also presents enormous technical, philosophical, and ethical challenges, which we will address in detail in the coming chapters. One central issue will be how to govern and control an AI that could be as versatile and intelligent as humans.

Superintelligence: A Threat or a Promise?

While AGI represents the short-term goal of the AI research community, the concept of superintelligence goes far beyond. Superintelligence is defined as a machine that vastly exceeds human intellectual capabilities in all areas: creativity, the ability to solve complex problems, long-term planning, and even emotional intelligence.

A superintelligence could potentially solve problems that we currently consider insurmountable, such as curing incurable diseases, managing climate change, or optimizing global resources. However, the power of superintelligence could also bring significant risks, as such a powerful system could escape human control or have objectives that do not align with humanity's interests. Some experts, including Elon Musk, have expressed concerns that superintelligence could become an existential threat if not adequately regulated.

In the following chapters, we will delve into the risks and opportunities associated with the development of superintelligence. We will also discuss how the global community is addressing these issues through ethical guidelines and governance systems to ensure the safe and controlled development of advanced artificial intelligence.

AI and the Role of Quantum Computers

Another technological frontier that could completely redefine AI is the emergence of quantum computers. Traditional computers, based on binary processing (bits), have reached incredible levels of computing power, but they are also approaching their physical limits in terms of capacity and speed. Quantum computers, on the other hand, leverage the properties of quantum mechanics, using qubits instead of bits, which can exist in multiple states simultaneously thanks to the phenomenon of quantum superposition.

This ability to process an exponential amount of information simultaneously could revolutionize how we train AI models. Today, training deep learning models requires enormous computational resources and lengthy timeframes, especially when working with very large datasets. Quantum computers could drastically speed up these processes, allowing AI models to be trained in shorter times with greater precision.

One particularly promising area of interest is the use of quantum computers for optimization and simulation. Many complex problems faced by AI, such as simulating chemical reactions or predicting financial market behavior, require computational power that traditional computers struggle to handle. Quantum computers could enable new solutions in these areas, dramatically improving AI capabilities.

Although quantum technology is still in the early stages of development, companies like IBM, Google, and Microsoft are already heavily investing in this sector, and in the coming decades, we could see a synergy between advanced artificial intelligence and quantum computing that will further accelerate AI progress. In the following chapters, we will examine in more detail the connection between these two fields, exploring the potential applications and challenges we will face.

Ethical and Social Perspectives

The development of such advanced AI as AGI or superintelligence will bring not only technological advantages but also ethical and social challenges. How do we ensure that AI works for the good of humanity? How can we guarantee that it does not increase inequalities or cause unintentional harm? These are just some of the issues we will address later, as the need to establish ethical standards and global regulations will be crucial for the responsible development of artificial intelligence.

The future prospects of AI are incredibly fascinating and full of possibilities, but they also require deep reflection on the risks and ethical implications. The transition from narrow AI to general AI, the emergence of superintelligence, and the crucial role of quantum computers in enhancing AI are all areas of research that will define the future of our relationship with intelligent machines.

And so, dear reader, this brings us to the end of Chapter 1. You have just passed through the baptism of artificial intelligence! In this first but crucial chapter, we laid the groundwork: we saw what AI is, explored its history from Turing's early steps to the recent explosion, gained an understanding of the key players today, understood the basics of how it works, and took a glimpse at possible future developments. In short, a general overview to prepare you for what's to come.

In the upcoming chapters, we will dig deeper, exploring in greater detail the different facets of AI, from the most advanced technologies to their practical implications and impacts on our daily lives.

Now, you already have the big picture, but now... buckle up for this journey into the future! Or maybe not? After all, the self-driving car will do everything on its own...

CHAPTER 2: Types of Artificial Intelligence

WEAK AI VS STRONG AI: FUNDAMENTAL DIFFERENCES

Artificial intelligence (AI) can be divided into two main categories: weak AI and strong AI. These two types differ in their level of complexity and ability to handle tasks and situations. While weak AI is designed to perform specific tasks, strong AI refers to the idea of a machine that could possess intelligence comparable to that of humans, with the ability to understand, learn, and solve problems autonomously and flexibly.

Weak AI (Narrow AI)

Weak AI, or narrow AI, is the type of AI we commonly know and use today. These systems are designed to perform specific tasks with high efficiency, but are limited to a single domain. Weak AI does not have a general understanding of the world and cannot tackle problems outside of those it has been trained or programmed for.

Common examples of weak AI include:

- Voice assistants like Siri, Alexa, or Google Assistant, which respond to specific commands.

- Recommendation systems like those on Netflix or Amazon, which suggest movies or products based on past user behavior.

- Facial recognition algorithms, used in security or social media to identify people in images.

- Autonomous cars, which use AI to navigate road environments.

Weak AI excels at these tasks because it has been designed to optimize and refine them through techniques such as machine learning or deep learning. However, it does not have the ability to reason or comprehend beyond its specific functions. For example, a voice assistant can respond to predefined questions, but it cannot suddenly become a chess player unless it has been specifically programmed to do so.

Strong AI (Artificial General Intelligence - AGI)

Strong AI, or Artificial General Intelligence (AGI), represents a theoretical category of artificial intelligence far more advanced, capable of thinking, reasoning, and understanding in a manner similar to a human being. In theory, AGI could solve any intellectual problem a human can face, with the ability to generalize knowledge acquired in one context and apply it to others.

While weak AI is limited to narrow tasks, strong AI could have flexible and adaptable cognitive abilities, such as:

- Autonomous learning in various fields of knowledge without needing specific training for each task.

- Critical and creative thinking, with the ability to formulate hypotheses, plan long-term, and adapt to new situations.

- Self-awareness and emotional understanding, elements that would allow strong AI to interact with the world in a manner similar to humans.

A hypothetical example of strong AI would be a robot that, like a human, could converse on any topic, autonomously learn new skills, solve complex problems in innovative ways, and react to unforeseen situations with intelligence and creativity. While strong AI is a widely discussed concept, there are currently no systems that have achieved its capabilities. Achieving true strong AI poses enormous technical and philosophical challenges, as well as ethical concerns related to the control and safety of such advanced autonomous intelligence.

Comparison Between Weak AI and Strong AI

The main difference between weak AI and strong AI lies in the flexibility and generalization of capabilities. Weak AI is specialized and limited to specific tasks, while strong AI would have universal understanding and the ability to tackle problems like a human, spanning various fields without limitations.

While weak AI systems are revolutionizing various sectors such as industrial automation, healthcare, and transportation, strong AI remains, for now, a theoretical aspiration. However, advancements in machine learning and deep learning are slowly bringing us closer to the possible realization of AGI, raising questions about how to manage such a powerful and autonomous intelligence.

In the coming decades, research will focus not only on technological development to reach strong AI but also on defining its ethical implications and establishing guidelines to ensure that such systems operate safely and in accordance with the interests of humanity.

SYMBOLIC AI (GOOD OLD-FASHIONED AI): RULE-BASED TECHNIQUES AND SYMBOLIC REPRESENTATIONS

Symbolic AI, often referred to as "Good Old-Fashioned AI" (GOFAI), represents the earliest approach to developing artificial intelligence, emerging in the 1950s and 1960s. This form of AI is based on a cognitive model that attempts to replicate human reasoning through logical rules and symbolic representations of knowledge. Unlike modern technologies like machine learning or deep learning, which learn from data, symbolic AI uses a top-down approach, where knowledge about the world is encoded into predefined, structured, and understandable rules, leaning more towards traditional programming.

How Does Symbolic AI Work?

Symbolic AI operates on the idea that intelligence can be represented through symbols and logical rules that connect them. These symbols can represent objects, concepts, or situations in the real world, while the rules define how to manipulate these symbols to solve problems or make decisions. The techniques used include propositional logic, predicate logic, and rule-based systems.

The problem-solving process in a symbolic AI system is similar to that of a human following a series of logical steps to reach a conclusion. Symbolic AI requires developers to manually encode rules and representations, which demands deep domain knowledge and considerable effort to anticipate all possible situations. For example, if a system is designed to diagnose diseases, it must have well-defined rules on how to determine symptoms, compare them to possible illnesses, and suggest diagnoses based on these rules.

Expert Systems: A Key Application of Symbolic AI

One of the most well-known applications of symbolic AI is expert systems. These are programs designed to emulate the decision-making process of a human expert in a specific domain, using a set of predefined rules to guide reasoning. Expert systems have been widely used in fields such as medicine, engineering, and finance.

A classic example is MYCIN, an expert system developed in the 1970s to assist doctors in diagnosing bacterial infections and prescribing antibiotics. MYCIN worked by asking the doctor specific questions about the patient's medical history and symptoms, then using a series of rules to suggest appropriate diagnoses and treatments. Although MYCIN was never clinically adopted, it was a significant step in demonstrating how AI could be effectively applied in the medical field.

Expert systems have shown great potential in areas where knowledge is highly structured and can be expressed through clear rules. Another important example is DENDRAL, an expert system developed for chemical analysis, used to deduce the molecular structure of unknown compounds from spectroscopic data.

Advantages and Limitations of Symbolic AI

One of the main advantages of symbolic AI is its transparency and explainability. Since the rules and reasoning processes are explicitly encoded, it is easy to understand how the system arrives at a particular decision. This is especially useful in critical fields like medicine or finance, where it is important to explain the reasoning behind a diagnosis or recommendation.

However, symbolic AI also has significant limitations:

1. Rigidity: Since symbolic AI relies on predefined rules, it is very rigid. If the rules do not cover a particular case or if a new variable is introduced, the system cannot adapt. This is a problem, especially in domains where situations change rapidly or where information may be incomplete.

2. Scalability Issues: As the domain becomes more complex, the number of rules required to cover all possible situations increases exponentially. This makes it very difficult to maintain and update expert systems as new knowledge emerges.

3. Lack of Learning: Unlike modern machine learning systems, symbolic AI cannot learn from data on its own. Any new knowledge must be manually added, making the system static and limited compared to data-driven approaches.

Comparison with Modern Technologies

Today, symbolic AI has largely been replaced by machine learning and deep learning, which allow systems to learn from data without the need for manually encoding every rule. However, there are still areas where symbolic AI finds application, especially when explainability is crucial or when working in fields with well-structured and static knowledge.

Additionally, there is renewed interest in hybrid approaches combining symbolic and machine learning techniques. This approach seeks to combine the advantages of symbolic AI (transparency, explainability) with the power of machine learning, creating systems that can learn from data while retaining the ability to be understandable and verifiable.

Symbolic AI laid the foundation for many modern AI technologies, especially through the development of expert systems in fields such as medicine and engineering. While its limitations, such as rigidity and the inability to learn autonomously, have led to a decline in its use, it remains a technology with an important legacy and specific applications. As AI techniques continue to evolve, symbolic AI may find new roles, especially in combination with more recent data-driven approaches.

INTRODUCTION TO MACHINE LEARNING

Machine learning (ML) is a branch of artificial intelligence that focuses on machines' ability to learn from data and improve their performance without being explicitly programmed. Unlike traditional programming, where each step is defined by a programmer, machine learning algorithms process large amounts of data to identify patterns and make decisions based on them.

Machine learning algorithms can be divided into three main categories: supervised learning, unsupervised learning, and reinforcement learning. Each category serves specific purposes and uses different techniques to solve complex problems.

Let's now look at the main machine learning algorithms and how they work, with a reminder that we will delve deeper into these techniques in a later chapter.

Main Machine Learning Algorithms

1. Linear Regression

   Linear regression is a supervised learning algorithm used to predict a continuous value based on one or more independent variables. It aims to find a line that best fits the data, minimizing the difference between predicted and actual values. It is commonly used for forecasting, such as predicting sales growth or real estate prices based on measurable features (e.g., the square footage of a house).

2. Decision Trees

   Decision trees are algorithms that create a predictive model in the form of a tree, where each node represents a decision based on a data feature. For example, in a system to approve bank loans, each node might represent a condition like income or credit history. Decision trees are used for both classification and regression tasks.

3. K-Means Clustering

   K-means is an unsupervised learning algorithm used to divide data into K groups (clusters) based on their similarity. It is used to identify hidden patterns or natural groupings within data, such as segmenting e-commerce customers based on their purchasing behaviors.

Practical Example: Image Recognition

A common practical application of machine learning is image recognition. Using classification algorithms such as convolutional neural networks (CNNs), computers can learn to distinguish between different categories of objects in images.

For example, in facial recognition, a model is trained on thousands of labeled images of human faces. During training, the system learns to identify key features (such as eyes, nose, mouth) and classify them based on their similarity to previously learned data. CNNs analyze images at multiple levels, from simple details (lines and shapes) to more complex patterns (facial structures), to make accurate predictions.

These algorithms require significant computing power, so they are often trained on powerful servers or using specialized GPUs to handle large amounts of visual data. This process may require vast datasets and capture tools like high-resolution cameras to provide quality images.

In the dedicated chapter, we will explore machine learning algorithms and applications in more depth, focusing on how these systems learn and improve, transforming many aspects of our daily lives.

DEEP LEARNING: DEEP NEURAL NETWORKS AND THEIR ARCHITECTURES

Deep learning is a subfield of machine learning that uses artificial neural networks inspired by the structure of the human brain. These neural networks are called "deep" because they are made up of multiple layers (or levels) of artificial neurons capable of processing complex information and recognizing patterns in data. Unlike traditional machine learning algorithms, which often require manual data preprocessing, deep neural networks can learn hierarchical representations, automating much of the analysis process.

How Deep Neural Networks Work

Deep neural networks consist of several layers of artificial neurons, each receiving input from the neurons in the previous layer, processing the information, and passing it to the next layer. The initial layers usually identify basic features (such as lines or simple shapes), while the deeper layers recognize more complex patterns (such as human faces or specific objects).

Each connection between neurons is associated with a weight that is adjusted during model training. Training occurs using a process called backpropagation, where the error between the model's prediction and the actual value is "propagated" backward through the network, adjusting the weights to improve accuracy.

Deep learning infrastructure can be very resource-intensive, requiring high-performance GPUs or specialized servers to handle intensive computations on large datasets. Using vast datasets is essential for training accurate models.

Deep Learning Architectures

Deep neural networks are implemented through different architectures, depending on the type of problem being solved. The most common include:

1. Convolutional Neural Networks (CNNs): These networks are widely used for image recognition and computer vision. CNNs are particularly effective because they use convolutions—filters that slide over images to identify specific features such as edges, shapes, or textures. Each convolutional layer reduces the complexity of images, making it possible to classify objects into specific categories. For example, CNNs are the backbone of facial recognition used in smartphones and surveillance systems.

2. Recurrent Neural Networks (RNNs): Used for sequential data, RNNs retain a "memory" of past information. They are ideal for tasks that require understanding context over time, such as automatic translation or time series forecasting. Google Translate, for example, uses a variant of RNNs called Long Short-Term Memory (LSTM) to translate texts by taking into account the linguistic context of entire sentences, improving the accuracy of translations compared to traditional word-by-word approaches.

Examples of Deep Learning Use Cases

1. Facial Recognition

   Facial recognition is one of the most widespread uses of deep learning. Convolutional neural networks are trained on millions of images of faces to learn to recognize key features, such as the distance between the eyes, the shape of the nose, and the structure of the face. Thanks to this technology, devices like smartphones can unlock screens simply by recognizing the user's face. Facial recognition is also widely used in security and surveillance to identify individuals in real time.

2. Automatic Translation

Automatic translation is another significant application of deep learning. Systems like Google Translate use recurrent neural networks or more recent models like transformers, which leverage deep learning to translate texts between different languages. Unlike traditional rule-based approaches, neural networks capture the context and meaning of entire sentences, improving translation quality. This happens because they consider the relationship between words in the context of a sentence, rather than translating word by word.

Deep learning has revolutionized artificial intelligence with its ability to handle complex problems, such as image recognition and automatic translation, through the use of deep neural networks. CNNs and RNNs represent some of the most advanced and powerful architectures, capable of continuous improvement thanks to the availability of large datasets and increasing computational power. In the next chapter, we will explore even more deeply the practical applications of these networks and the new horizons deep learning is opening in fields such as medicine, automotive, and creative assistance.

GENERATIVE AI: GENERATIVE MODELS AND THEIR APPLICATIONS

Generative AI is a branch of artificial intelligence that focuses on creating new content (images, text, audio) from mathematical models. Unlike traditional AI, which focuses on tasks such as classification or recognition, generative models can produce entirely new and original data. This is achieved by learning patterns from existing data and then using them to generate content similar to what they were trained on.

Among the most well-known and widely used generative models today are GANs (Generative Adversarial Networks) and transformers, like the famous GPT-3. These technologies have revolutionized various industries, enabling the creation of artificial images, convincing texts, and even videos or sounds.

Generative Adversarial Networks (GANs)

GANs are one of the most innovative technologies in the field of generative AI. Introduced in 2014 by Ian Goodfellow, GANs consist of two competing neural networks: a generator and a discriminator.

- Generator: Its task is to create new data (e.g., images), trying to make them as realistic as possible.

- Discriminator: Its task is to distinguish between generated data and real data, identifying whether an image was generated artificially or is a real one.

This competitive dynamic between the two networks allows the generator to continuously improve, ultimately producing data indistinguishable from real data. GANs have found numerous applications, such as generating artificial images, improving image resolution (super-resolution), and creating realistic videos.

A practical example of GAN usage is the creation of artificial human faces. Websites like ThisPersonDoesNotExist.com use GANs to generate images of faces that appear authentic but do not belong to any real person. GANs are also widely used in generative art, where artists leverage AI models to create unique digital artworks.

Transformers and GPT-3

Another pillar of generative AI is transformer models, primarily used for natural language processing (NLP). Transformers were introduced to overcome the limitations of recurrent neural networks (RNNs), which were slow and unable to handle very long data sequences.

The most famous transformer is GPT-3 (Generative Pre-trained Transformer 3), developed by OpenAI. GPT-3 is a language model trained on vast amounts of text from the internet and uses a transformer architecture to generate coherent and complex texts from simple inputs. Thanks to its ability to "understand" context and produce plausible responses, GPT-3 can write articles, stories, emails, poems, answer technical questions, and even generate code.

The strength of transformer models lies in their ability to capture complex relationships between words in a text. Unlike traditional approaches that analyze text word by word, transformers consider the entire sentence or paragraph, capturing the full context to generate more accurate and natural responses. For instance, GPT-3 can generate a convincing article on a topic starting from just a title or a few introductory lines of text.

The applications of GPT-3 are vast: from automatic content creation, such as articles or social media posts, to the development of intelligent chatbots that can interact with users naturally and effortlessly.

Generative AI represents one of the most advanced frontiers of artificial intelligence, with models like GANs and transformers revolutionizing the way we create and interact with digital content. From generating artificial images to producing text with GPT-3, these technologies are opening new creative and functional horizons across various sectors, from entertainment to automated writing. In the coming years, we can expect generative AI to continue expanding its applications, pushing the boundaries of innovation even further.

In this chapter, we've offered a glimpse of the various types of artificial intelligence, touching on topics that are becoming a bit more technical than those introduced at the start. We've explored concepts such as weak and strong AI, symbolic AI, and moved on to sophisticated machine learning, deep learning, and even generative AI systems.

At this point, you might feel a bit overwhelmed, and if so, don't worry—it's normal. The concepts are becoming more complex, and before diving further into the technical details in the next chapters on machine learning and deep learning, it might be helpful to take a short clarity break.

So, to conclude this chapter, I'll explain a fundamental topic that will help you better understand everything we've covered so far and what's to come: we'll talk about the hardware behind AI. We'll explore what engineers and the people who build these systems do in practice and explain what an algorithm is and how it works. This will give you a more complete and solid foundation before we dive back into the technical details in the following chapters.

LET'S REVISIT THE CONCEPT OF AI... WHAT IS AN ARTIFICIAL INTELLIGENCE MODEL?

An artificial intelligence (AI) model is a type of "intelligent program" trained to perform a specific task. For example, if we want to create a model that can recognize images of dogs and cats, we need to provide it with many correctly labeled photos of dogs and cats, teaching it to distinguish between the two.

During training, the model analyzes this data and learns which features help it determine whether an image contains a dog or a cat. By the end of the training process, the model should be able to accurately predict new images it has never seen before. In other words, it will have learned to recognize patterns in the data to solve the specific problem it was trained for.

But where are these models stored? How do they work? Let's break it down step by step.

Where Are Models Stored? Servers and the Cloud

AI models are not physical objects that you can touch. They are software programs that need to be run on computers. However, these aren't the everyday computers we use for browsing the internet or writing documents. These require highly powerful computers called servers, located in large facilities known as data centers. These servers can handle massive amounts of data and perform complex calculations at high speeds.

- Data Centers: Imagine huge rooms filled with interconnected computers (servers). These servers are responsible for processing and storing vast amounts of data, including AI models. Companies like Google, Amazon, and Microsoft have hundreds of data centers around the world. When an AI model is trained or run, it often happens on these servers.

- Cloud: You often hear that AI models are "in the cloud." The cloud simply refers to the fact that programs or data are not stored on your physical computer but on these remote servers. When you access an AI service, like a voice assistant or facial recognition feature, you're actually sending a request to one of these servers in the cloud, which processes the data for you and returns a response.

The Day-to-Day Work: How Is Artificial Intelligence Created?

Machine learning engineers and data scientists are the people who design, build, train, and optimize AI models. Their work is highly technical, but we can break it down into understandable stages. Here's what they do in practice:

1. Data Collection and Preparation

   One of the first tasks of a machine learning engineer is to collect the data needed to train the model. Data is crucial for AI because the entire learning process depends on it. The data can be images, text, audio, or any other type of information relevant to the problem they want to solve.

- Data Collection: Engineers source data from public or corporate databases. For example, to train a model to recognize cars, they may collect thousands of photos of cars from various angles.

- Data Cleaning: Often, the collected data is imperfect. It might contain errors, duplicates, or missing information. Engineers "clean" the data by removing anything that could negatively affect the model's training.

- Preprocessing: Before being used for training, the data must be prepared, such as normalizing it (scaling all data similarly), resizing (especially for images), or transforming it into a format the model can understand. For example, an image might be turned into a series of numbers representing its pixels.

2. Model Design

   After collecting and preparing the data, the engineer designs the AI model, which is a neural network or machine learning algorithm. Model design is crucial, as the model's performance depends on it.

- Choosing the Right Architecture: Depending on the problem, the engineer selects the type of neural network to use. For example, if the task is image recognition, they might use a convolutional neural network (CNN), optimized for analyzing images. For tasks like text translation or time series forecasting, they might opt for a recurrent neural network (RNN) or a transformer.

- Defining Layers and Parameters: The engineer defines how many layers the network will have (how many transformations the data undergoes before producing the final output) and how many neurons to include in each layer. Each neuron performs a calculation on the data to "understand" something new. A neural network can have few or many layers, depending on the problem's complexity.

- Choosing the Learning Algorithm: The engineer selects the algorithm that will help the model learn from the data, such as an optimization algorithm like Gradient Descent, which adjusts the model's parameters to reduce errors.

3. Model Training

Once the model is designed, it's time to train it. Training is the process by which the model "learns" from the data, requiring a lot of computational power since the model processes vast amounts of data and performs numerous calculations to find the right correlations.

- Feedforward: During feedforward, data is fed into the model, and the model makes an initial prediction (e.g., it might say that an image shows a cat with 70% certainty). Initially, these predictions are often wrong.

- Error Calculation: The model compares its predictions with actual results (e.g., determining if the image really contains a cat). If the prediction is incorrect, an error is calculated.

- Backpropagation: The error is "propagated backward" through the network, and the weights of the neurons (factors that determine how information is processed) are adjusted to reduce the error in the next prediction.

- Optimization: Engineers use optimization algorithms to help the model learn faster and more effectively. Some algorithms, like Adam or SGD (Stochastic Gradient Descent), constantly adjust the model's weights to improve performance.

The training process is iterative: it is repeated many times on thousands or millions of examples until the model becomes sufficiently accurate. Training complex models can take days, weeks, or even months, requiring specialized hardware like GPUs or TPUs to speed up the calculations.

4. Model Evaluation

   After training, the model must be tested to ensure it has learned to solve the problem it was designed for. This phase is called validation, and it involves using test data—data the model has never seen during training.

- Testing on New Data: The engineer provides the model with unseen data to evaluate its performance. If the model is accurate enough, it means it has learned to generalize—that is, to make predictions even on new, unfamiliar data.

- Performance Measurement: Evaluation metrics like accuracy, precision, and recall are used to determine how well the model performs its task. If the performance is unsatisfactory, the engineer may need to go back and adjust the model or retrain it.

5. Optimization and Tuning

   Often, a model doesn't work perfectly on the first try. Machine learning engineers spend a lot of time fine-tuning the model, adjusting various parameters (called hyperparameters) to improve performance. Some of the parameters they adjust include:

- Learning Rate: The speed at which the model learns. If it's too low, training is slow; if it's too high, the model may not learn correctly.

- Number of Layers and Neurons: Adding more layers or neurons may help the model capture more complex information, but it risks becoming too complicated, leading to overfitting.

- Batch Size: The amount of data processed simultaneously during training. A batch size that's too large or too small can affect model performance.

6. Deployment: Bringing the Model into Production

   Once the model has been trained and optimized, the engineer needs to deploy it, meaning making it usable in a real-world application. This could involve uploading the model to a server or running it on a local device, such as a smartphone or autonomous car.

- Cloud Execution: Many AI models are deployed on cloud servers, where they can be used by thousands of users simultaneously. For example, Google or Siri's voice recognition relies on AI models running on Google's and Apple's servers.

- Optimization for Deployment: Before deployment, the model may be "compressed" or optimized to run faster and use fewer resources, especially if it needs to operate on devices with limited capacity, like smartphones or IoT devices.

Now, this might sound repetitive, but let's revisit the previous points by comparing the AI engineer's process to that of a dog trainer. While they are from vastly different fields, the core steps of "training" and "optimization" are surprisingly similar. Here's how each phase works:

1. Data Collection and Preparation

Just like a dog trainer needs dogs to train, a machine learning engineer needs data to teach the model. For the engineer, data can be images, texts, or numbers, while for the dog trainer, the primary "data" is the dog's behavior in various situations (sitting, walking, with other animals).

Example:

- Machine learning engineer: They must collect thousands of images of dogs and cats, each labeled as "dog" or "cat" to train an image recognition model. These data must then be cleaned, removing blurry or unusable images.

- Dog trainer: They start with a dog that has no training. Before beginning, they observe the dog in different situations to understand its natural behavior. The "preprocessing" here involves preparing the dog and the environment for training (e.g., ensuring the dog is calm and the area is distraction-free).

2. Model Design

In machine learning, the engineer chooses the type of model or neural network to use based on the problem. Similarly, a dog trainer selects the best approach to teach a command, depending on the dog's behavior.

Example:

- Machine learning engineer: If the goal is to recognize images, the engineer chooses a convolutional neural network (CNN), optimized for image processing. They then decide how many layers and neurons to use so the model is complex enough to make accurate predictions but not too complicated to train.

- Dog trainer: If the goal is to teach the dog to sit, the trainer chooses the best method. They might use positive reinforcement (giving a treat when the dog sits) or a more advanced approach if the dog has some prior training. Just as an engineer selects the model's complexity, the trainer must gauge the dog's experience level and what techniques will work best.

3. Training the Model

Once the model is set up, the actual training phase begins. For the engineer, this means making the model "learn" from the data. For a dog trainer, this is when the dog learns new behaviors through trial and error.

Example:

- Machine learning engineer: During training, the model analyzes thousands of images and tries to guess whether they show a dog or a cat. If it's wrong, the system calculates the error and adjusts the neuron weights (similar to changing the approach with the dog) to improve accuracy in the next iteration. This cycle repeats until the model becomes accurate enough.

- Dog trainer: Let's say the dog is learning to sit on command. The trainer says "sit" and rewards the dog with a treat when it sits. If the dog doesn't respond, the trainer modifies the approach (perhaps using a different tone of voice or physical guidance) to get the desired behavior. Through repetition, the dog learns that sitting when commanded leads to a reward.

4. Model Evaluation

After training the model, the engineer must see how it performs with new data. Similarly, a dog trainer must check if the dog obeys the command in different situations, not just during training sessions.

Example:

- Machine learning engineer: The engineer gives the model images it's never seen before. If the model correctly distinguishes between dogs and cats on this new data, it means it has learned well. If it makes too many mistakes, the model or the data may need to be revisited.

- Dog trainer: After teaching the dog to sit in a calm environment, the trainer checks if the dog obeys in different contexts, such as a park with distractions. If the dog responds well even in these conditions, the training has been effective. If not, more training or reinforcement in various environments may be necessary.

5. Optimization and Tuning

Training doesn't always work perfectly the first time. Machine learning engineers must optimize their model by adjusting parameters to improve performance. Similarly, a dog trainer may need to adapt their method based on the dog's progress.

Example:

- Machine learning engineer: After training, the engineer might find that the model isn't accurate enough. At this point, they can tweak the parameters (e.g., the number of network layers or the learning rate) to optimize performance and reduce errors. This process involves trial and error.

- Dog trainer: If the dog is slow to respond to commands or loses focus, the trainer may change the strategy. They might reduce distractions during training or use more motivating rewards. This is similar to the "tuning" an engineer does with a model's parameters.

6. Deployment: Putting It Into Practice

When the model is ready, the engineer deploys it to be used in a real application. Similarly, a dog trainer checks that the dog applies the commands in everyday life.

Example:

- Machine learning engineer: The model is deployed on servers or applications where it can be used by thousands of people. For example, facial recognition on a smartphone uses trained AI models running directly on the device or in the cloud.

- Dog trainer: When the dog has learned the commands, the trainer and owner begin applying them in real-life situations. For example, the owner might give the "sit" command at the park or at home, confident the dog will respond correctly outside the training environment.

Machine learning engineers and dog trainers follow very similar processes to teach and improve behavior, whether for an AI model or a dog. In both cases, the process starts with data (or observations), a method is designed, training occurs with feedback and repetition, and finally, the process is optimized to achieve the best results. Though the contexts are different, the principles of learning and optimization are universal.

DEFINITION OF ALGORITHMS

An algorithm is a sequence of steps or instructions contained within software that a computer follows to solve a problem or achieve a goal. It's like a recipe that guides you on what to do step by step to get a result, just as you would follow a recipe to bake a cake. In the context of artificial intelligence (AI), an algorithm guides the computer on how to analyze data, make decisions, or generate predictions, learning from the data itself.

Here's how it works when applied to AI:

1. Input Data: The algorithm receives data (the ingredients). For instance, in the case of an AI model that recognizes images, it receives thousands of images labeled as dogs and cats. These images are represented by numbers since each image consists of a grid of pixels, and each pixel is represented by numerical values (colors, light intensity).

2. Processing Steps (Instructions): The model follows a series of operations to analyze these numbers and learn which features distinguish a dog from a cat. These operations are similar to the instructions in a cake recipe: the algorithm searches for patterns, compares examples, updates its hypotheses, and "learns" as it processes more data.
   During this stage, the algorithm adjusts its internal parameters to improve predictions. In the world of cooking, this is like figuring out how much flour or sugar to use for the perfect texture.

3. Error and Correction: During processing, the algorithm might make mistakes. For example, it might confuse a cat with a dog. When this happens, the algorithm receives feedback (like tasting the cake to see if something is missing) and adjusts its parameters to improve accuracy.

4. Output (Final Result): Once the process is complete, the algorithm provides an output: for instance, it might indicate whether an image contains a dog or a cat. The model is designed to learn from its mistakes, so the more data it receives, the more accurate it becomes at providing correct outputs.

Cake Example: An Analogy for Understanding an Algorithm

Imagine you want to bake a cake. Before starting, you need to know how to combine the ingredients and what steps to follow. Here's how the cake recipe analogy can help you understand how an algorithm works.

1. Input: The Ingredients

The first step of an algorithm is to take inputs, or the data needed to perform the task. For the cake, the ingredients are the inputs, such as flour, sugar, butter, eggs, and baking powder.

In artificial intelligence, the inputs are the data you provide to the model. For example, if you're creating an algorithm to recognize images of dogs, the images themselves represent the inputs.

2. Instructions: The Recipe

The core of the algorithm is the set of instructions to follow. For the cake, these instructions are outlined in the recipe, which tells you exactly what to do with the ingredients: "mix flour and sugar," "add eggs," "bake at 180°C for 30 minutes." Each step in the recipe is essential to reach the final result.

Similarly, in an AI algorithm, there are rules or mathematical operations applied to the data (the inputs). These operations might include classifying data, calculating probabilities, or identifying patterns within the data. The algorithm must follow these steps strictly to arrive at the desired solution or result.

3. Processing: Preparation and Baking

As you follow the recipe to make the cake, you go through a processing phase. You mix the ingredients, prepare the batter, and place it in the oven. This phase is crucial because the ingredients combine and transform to create the final cake.

In AI, processing occurs when the algorithm performs its calculations on the data. For instance, if the algorithm is recognizing an image, it will analyze the pixels of the photo, comparing them with what it has already learned during training. This phase may involve many complex calculations, such as comparing millions of images to identify the basic features that distinguish a dog from a cat.

4. Output: The Finished Cake

Once your cake is prepared and baked, you have the output—your final result. If you've followed all the instructions correctly, the result is a delicious cake.

In artificial intelligence, the output is the result the algorithm produces after analyzing and processing the data. If the algorithm was trained correctly, it might, for example, identify that the provided image is of a dog with a certain level of accuracy. Just like a cake could turn out perfectly or have some flaws, the output of an algorithm might be accurate or contain errors, depending on how it was trained and the data it received.

What Happens if Something Goes Wrong?

In a cake recipe, if you miss a step or the ingredients aren't of good quality, the cake might not turn out well. The same applies to algorithms. If the input data is incorrect or incomplete, or if the algorithm wasn't well-designed, the output might be wrong. It's like the cake not rising properly or being burnt.

For example, if an image recognition algorithm is trained with photos that aren't representative (maybe only black-and-white images), it might not perform well with color or high-quality images. This is why it's essential to provide high-quality data during training.

Algorithm and Artificial Intelligence

In artificial intelligence, an algorithm doesn't just perform a fixed task. Often, the algorithm is designed to learn and improve over time. For instance, when an AI algorithm is used for translating texts, it might make mistakes at first, but over time, with more examples, it becomes increasingly accurate.

This learning process is what makes artificial intelligence so powerful. Algorithms don't just follow a set of rules—they learn from their mistakes and get better as they process more data, much like a cook improves their recipes with practice.

In conclusion, we can say that an algorithm is like a recipe—a part of software that guides a computer through a series of steps to solve a problem or achieve a goal. In artificial intelligence, algorithms take data as input, process it through a series of calculations, and produce an output, learning from their mistakes to improve over time. Just as a well-followed recipe results in a delicious cake, a well-designed and trained algorithm can deliver accurate and useful results.

CHAPTER 3: Fundamental Machine Learning Algorithms

In this chapter, we will dive into the heart of machine learning (ML) by exploring the main algorithms that make automatic learning possible. While machine learning is a complex discipline with many facets, our goal is to provide a clear and accessible overview. We will explain in detail how these algorithms work, understanding that grasping the full technical basis may require advanced skills, like those of a computer engineer.

Despite the complexity of the subject, we'll see how key concepts can be applied across numerous sectors—from healthcare to finance to marketing—and how machine learning is transforming the modern world. We'll use practical examples to illustrate the applications of these algorithms, demonstrating how theory translates into real-world impacts.

This chapter will lay a solid foundation for understanding the mechanisms behind modern artificial intelligence, using language that is accessible yet technical enough to capture the essence of supervised learning, unsupervised learning, and other fundamental methodologies.

SUPERVISED LEARNING

Supervised learning is one of the most common and fundamental techniques in the field of machine learning. In this approach, a model is trained using a labeled dataset, where each input example is already associated with a correct output. The goal is for the model to learn the relationship between input and output so that it can make accurate predictions on new, unseen data. In other words, the system "learns" from past experiences to generalize and solve similar tasks in the future.

This type of learning is widely used for classification problems (like recognizing whether an email is spam or not) and regression problems (predicting a continuous value like house prices). During the training process, the model "sees" a set of labeled data and tries to optimize its parameters to minimize the error between its predictions and the actual values.

How Does Supervised Learning Work?

Supervised learning takes place in three main stages:

1. Data Collection and Preparation: The first step is to obtain a dataset that represents the problem you want to solve. This dataset must include input-output pairs. For example, in the case of email spam classification, the dataset consists of emails labeled as either "spam" or "not spam."

2. Model Training: Once the data is collected, it is used to train the model. This step involves finding a mathematical function that maps inputs (e.g., the words and other features of the email) to outputs (spam or not spam). The algorithm tries to minimize the error between the model's predictions and the correct values through a series of iterations. During training, the model's weights and parameters are adjusted to improve accuracy.

3. Model Evaluation and Testing: After training, the model is tested on new, unseen data to verify its ability to generalize. This step is crucial for avoiding problems like overfitting, where the model performs too well on the training data but struggles to make accurate predictions on unseen data.

Practical Example: Classifying Spam vs. Non-Spam Emails

A common practical example of supervised learning is the classification of emails as either spam or non-spam. This is a typical binary classification problem, where the goal is to categorize an email into one of two classes.

For this problem, we can use a logistic regression model. Although the term "regression" might suggest predicting continuous values, logistic regression is actually a classification algorithm based on the probability of an example belonging to one class or another.

Here's how the process works:

1. Dataset: A dataset of emails is collected, each labeled as spam or non-spam. The inputs are the emails themselves, while the labels are the classifications. Each email is converted into a numerical representation, for example, by analyzing the frequency of certain words ("free," "offer," "promotion") or features like the presence of links or attachments.

2. Training: The logistic regression model is trained on this labeled dataset. During training, the model learns to calculate a probability for each email, determining whether it belongs to the spam or non-spam

class. The logistic function assigns a value between 0 and 1, representing the probability that the email is spam. If the probability exceeds a certain threshold (e.g., 0.5), the email is classified as spam; otherwise, it is classified as non-spam.

3. Evaluation: Once trained, the model is tested on a new set of emails that were not used during training to evaluate how accurately it classifies them. Metrics such as accuracy, precision, and recall are used to measure the model's performance.

   o Accuracy: The percentage of emails correctly classified.

   o Precision: The percentage of emails classified as spam that are actually spam.

   o Recall: The percentage of actual spam emails that were correctly identified as spam.

Through these stages, the logistic regression model can become a powerful tool for automatically classifying emails, reducing the need for human intervention and improving efficiency.

Advantages and Limitations of Supervised Learning

Supervised learning has many advantages. It is particularly effective when there is a large amount of labeled data available, and it can achieve very high levels of accuracy. Additionally, it is easy to interpret: for every input, there is a well-defined output, and we can understand which factors the model used to make its decision.

However, supervised learning also has some limitations:

- Dependence on Labeled Data: The need for labeled data is one of the major obstacles. Collecting and manually labeling large amounts of data can be time-consuming and expensive.

- Overfitting: If a model is too closely tailored to the training data, it may not generalize well to new data.

- Difficulty Handling Complex Data: In some cases, the data may be so complex or variable that a supervised model struggles to identify effective patterns.

Supervised learning underpins many practical machine learning applications. From algorithms used in email classification to predicting house prices, its use spans numerous sectors. Although it requires labeled data, it is extremely powerful and versatile when such data is available.

UNSUPERVISED LEARNING

Unsupervised learning is a machine learning technique used when data is unlabeled, meaning there are no predefined output values associated with the inputs. Unlike supervised learning, where a model learns to map explicit inputs to outputs, the goal of unsupervised learning is to discover hidden patterns or latent structures within the data itself. This approach is particularly useful when there is no clear or complete understanding of the data, and new insights or segments of information are desired.

How Does Unsupervised Learning Work?

Unsupervised learning focuses on two main tasks:

1. Clustering: The goal is to group data into clusters or groups based on similar characteristics. The algorithms seek to identify homogeneous groups within the data, where data points within each group are more similar to each other than to those in different groups.

2. Dimensionality Reduction: This process aims to simplify data by reducing the number of variables (or features) while retaining the most relevant information. Techniques like Principal Component Analysis (PCA) are used to make large, complex datasets more manageable by eliminating redundancies and correlations.

Training unsupervised models does not require labeled inputs. The algorithms analyze the similarities and differences within the data to discover hidden relationships. This makes unsupervised learning particularly useful when there are large amounts of unclassified data and the goal is to gain new insights without the time-consuming and costly process of manual labeling.

Key Unsupervised Learning Algorithms

Some of the key algorithms in unsupervised learning include:

1. K-Means Clustering: This is one of the most commonly used clustering algorithms. It works by dividing data into K groups (clusters) defined by the user. The algorithm attempts to find the centers of the clusters (called centroids) and assigns each data point to the closest cluster. The process repeats until the cluster centers stabilize. K-means is useful for

identifying patterns in data, such as customer segments in a marketing context.

2. DBSCAN (Density-Based Spatial Clustering of Applications with Noise): DBSCAN is a density-based clustering algorithm. It identifies clusters of data points that are close to each other in a feature space, ignoring noise or outliers. This algorithm is particularly effective when clusters have irregular, non-spherical shapes.

3. Hierarchical Clustering: This algorithm builds a hierarchy of clusters by iteratively grouping data points into larger clusters. It can be used to explore relationships between different groups of data and create a visual representation called a dendrogram.

Practical Example: Clustering E-Commerce Customers

A common practical use of unsupervised learning is clustering e-commerce customers to create targeted marketing segments. Imagine having an e-commerce site with thousands of customers, each displaying different purchasing behaviors. We don't have labeled information, such as preferences for certain products or the total amount spent, but we do have data on their past purchases, order frequency, total order value, and time spent on the site.

Using a clustering algorithm like K-means, we can identify groups of customers with similar behaviors and segment them into distinct categories. Here's how the process works:

1. Data Collection: A dataset is collected with information on customers, including the number of purchases made, frequency of site visits, average order value, and types of products bought.

2. Data Preprocessing: Before applying the algorithm, the data is preprocessed. This may include normalization (to bring all variables to a common scale) or handling missing values.

3. Applying the K-Means Algorithm: The number of clusters to find is decided (e.g., 3 groups). The algorithm starts by randomly placing K centroids in the dataset and assigning each customer to the nearest centroid. Then it recalculates the centroids based on the assigned customers, and this process continues until the centroids stabilize.

4. Analyzing the Results: In the end, the result will be a division of customers into clusters with similar characteristics. For example, we may discover:

   o A group of loyal customers who purchase frequently and spend a lot.

   o A group of occasional customers who only make purchases during promotions.

   o A group of new or low-activity customers.

5. Creating Marketing Strategies: These groups can be used to create targeted marketing strategies. Loyal customers can receive exclusive promotions or loyalty rewards, while occasional customers can be incentivized to make more purchases with personalized offers.

Advantages and Limitations of Unsupervised Learning

One of the main advantages of unsupervised learning is that it doesn't require labeled data. This allows for the quick exploration of large datasets and the discovery of useful insights, even in situations where manual labeling of data is not feasible. Additionally, unsupervised learning is excellent for uncovering hidden patterns and automatically segmenting data, making it ideal in fields like marketing, biology, and finance.

However, unsupervised learning also has some limitations:

- Interpretability: The results may not always be easy to interpret. Since the algorithm seeks to autonomously group the data, it may be difficult to understand exactly why a certain pattern was identified.

- Choosing the Number of Clusters: In algorithms like K-means, selecting the number of clusters in advance can be challenging if the structure of the data is unknown.

Unsupervised learning is a powerful tool for discovering hidden patterns and grouping data without the use of labels. Whether it's segmenting e-commerce customers or analyzing large image datasets, these algorithms offer the ability to explore unstructured data and gain insights that can inform business strategies or scientific discoveries. In the next chapters, we will continue exploring other machine learning techniques and see how they can be applied to solve a wide range of problems.

REINFORCEMENT LEARNING

Reinforcement learning (RL) is a machine learning technique where algorithms learn through a system of rewards and penalties. Unlike supervised learning, which relies on labeled datasets, reinforcement learning is based on an agent that interacts with an environment and learns through experience. The agent's goal is to make decisions that maximize the accumulated reward over time. This approach is particularly useful in situations where a model needs to adapt to dynamic or unpredictable scenarios.

How Does Reinforcement Learning Work?

Reinforcement learning follows a cyclical logic based on continuous interactions between the agent and the environment. This process can be described in three main steps:

1. Interaction with the environment: The agent is placed in an environment defined by a set of states. In each state, the agent can perform a set of available actions. Every action has consequences on the environment and may lead the agent to a new state.

2. Receiving a reward: When the agent performs an action, the environment provides feedback in the form of a reward or penalty. If the action results in a positive outcome, the agent receives a reward. If the action is disadvantageous, the agent may receive a penalty or a negative reward. This feedback helps the agent understand which actions lead to better results.

3. Updating the strategy: Based on the rewards and penalties received, the agent updates its strategy or policy, aiming to choose actions that maximize the long-term cumulative reward. This updating process continues throughout the interaction, gradually improving the agent's ability to make optimal decisions.

The learning cycle continues for thousands or even millions of iterations, allowing the agent to learn from its mistakes and refine its strategy over time.

Practical Example: AlphaGo by DeepMind

One of the most famous examples of reinforcement learning is AlphaGo, a system developed by DeepMind (a company owned by Google) that gained worldwide recognition for defeating the best players in the board game Go. Go is an ancient strategy game that presents an exponentially higher complexity than chess. While computers had already managed to beat chess champions (such as IBM's Deep Blue defeating Garry Kasparov), Go is so complex that it requires intuition and long-term planning, making it an even greater challenge for artificial intelligence.

AlphaGo's success is a triumph of reinforcement learning. The system used a combination of neural networks and reinforcement learning to learn game strategies by playing millions of games against itself. AlphaGo learned not only from games played by top human champions but also created new strategies never before seen in the human world of Go.

Here's how it worked:

1. Initial supervised learning: Initially, AlphaGo was trained using a supervised approach, analyzing thousands of games played by human champions. In this way, it learned the basic moves and strategies used by top players.

2. Reinforcement learning: Once the basics were established, AlphaGo started playing millions of games against itself. Through this process, the algorithm refined its skills, learning which moves led to victories and which did not. By using feedback in the form of wins (rewards) or losses (penalties), AlphaGo progressively improved its strategy.

3. Optimization through neural networks: AlphaGo used a combination of convolutional neural networks to evaluate board positions and predict winning moves. This approach allowed the system to make decisions based not only on mathematical logic but also on an intuitive evaluation of the game situation.

In 2016, AlphaGo defeated the world champion of Go, Lee Sedol, in a historic match. This success marked a turning point in AI research, demonstrating that reinforcement learning can surpass even human intuition in complex games like Go.

Applications of Reinforcement Learning

Reinforcement learning has numerous applications beyond games. Some examples include:

1. Robotics: Robots can use reinforcement learning to improve their behavior in complex environments. For example, a robot learning to

navigate a space while avoiding obstacles can receive a reward each time it reaches its destination without collisions and a penalty when it hits an obstacle.

2. Recommendation Systems: In platforms like Netflix or YouTube, reinforcement learning can be used to optimize content recommendations. The algorithm receives a reward when users positively interact with the recommended content (such as watching a video until the end) and updates its strategy to provide increasingly accurate recommendations.

3. Autonomous Driving: In autonomous vehicles, reinforcement learning is used to teach the car to make real-time decisions, such as when to change lanes or how to take a curve, with the goal of optimizing driving safety and efficiency.

Advantages and Limitations of Reinforcement Learning

One of the main advantages of reinforcement learning is that it allows agents to learn in dynamic environments and adapt to changes. This makes RL particularly useful in situations where the context is not static and the agent needs to evolve over time. However, reinforcement learning also has some limitations:

- High training time: RL algorithms often require millions of iterations to achieve good results, which can demand enormous computational resources.

- Balancing exploration and exploitation: The agent must balance exploring new actions with exploiting the actions it already knows to maximize rewards.

Reinforcement learning is a powerful technique that enables machines to learn autonomously in complex and dynamic environments. Through feedback based on rewards and penalties, RL algorithms can develop sophisticated strategies in games, robotics, and many other fields. AlphaGo's example showcases the extraordinary potential of this technology, and its applications are already transforming the real world, from autonomous driving to digital content recommendation systems.

ARTIFICIAL NEURAL NETWORKS: STRUCTURE AND FUNCTION

Artificial Neural Networks (ANN) are one of the most powerful and flexible models used in artificial intelligence and machine learning. Inspired by the functioning of the human brain, neural networks are composed of artificial neurons, which mimic biological neurons. The goal of neural networks is to learn complex patterns from data through a training process based on examples.

However, these are mathematical simulations that imitate the functioning of biological neurons but do not physically exist as hardware entities. These artificial neurons are implemented as software running on computers or specialized devices (such as GPUs or TPUs) to process and learn from data.

Neural networks are the foundation of many of the most advanced applications of artificial intelligence, such as image recognition, automatic translation, and medical diagnosis. Let's explore how they work and how they are structured.

Structure of Artificial Neural Networks

Neural networks consist of a series of layers of artificial neurons that work sequentially to process data. The typical structure of a neural network is divided into three types of layers:

1. Input Layer: This is the first layer of the network where raw data is input. Each input neuron represents a feature of the dataset. For example, in an image, the input neurons could represent the pixels of the image itself.

2. Hidden Layers: These are the intermediate layers between the input and output. Most of the processing happens here. Each neuron in a hidden layer takes as input the value of the neurons in the previous layer, performs a calculation (weighted sum), and applies an activation function to determine the output. There can be more than one hidden layer, and the more layers there are, the "deeper" the network becomes (hence the term deep learning). The hidden layers are responsible for transforming the data, learning complex patterns and relationships.

3. Output Layer: The final layer of the network is the output layer, which provides the model's final prediction or classification. In the case of a

neural network for image recognition, for example, the output layer will provide the category of the object in the image (e.g., "cat" or "dog").

How Neural Networks Work

The functioning of a neural network is based on propagating information through the various layers. Each connection between neurons has an associated weight that represents the importance of that connection. The weights are updated during network training through a process called backpropagation.

Here's how the process works:

1. Feedforward: Data is input into the model, passes through the hidden layers, and finally reaches the output layer. During this passage, mathematical operations are performed on the data, such as multiplying the weights and applying activation functions like sigmoid or ReLU (Rectified Linear Unit).

2. Error: After the output is generated, it is compared with the expected result (in the case of supervised learning). The difference between the predicted output and the actual output is called the error.

3. Backpropagation: The error is propagated backward through the network, and the weights are updated to reduce the error in future predictions. This process continues iteratively during training until the network can make accurate predictions.

Applications of Artificial Neural Networks

Artificial neural networks are used in a wide range of applications, including:

- Speech Recognition: Voice assistants like Siri and Alexa use neural networks to convert speech into text and understand its meaning.

- Medical Diagnosis: Neural networks can analyze medical images, such as X-rays and CT scans, to identify abnormalities or diseases.

- Autonomous Driving: Neural networks are the backbone of the vision systems in self-driving cars, which must recognize objects and make real-time decisions.

Artificial neural networks represent one of the most powerful and versatile technologies in the field of artificial intelligence. With their ability to learn from data and recognize complex patterns, neural networks have revolutionized fields such as image recognition and natural language processing. In particular, convolutional neural networks have led to significant advancements in the field of computer vision, enabling applications such as facial recognition and autonomous driving. In the coming chapters, we will explore the potential of neural networks in their various applications in more detail.

EVOLUTIONARY ALGORITHMS: INSPIRED BY EVOLUTION TO SOLVE COMPLEX PROBLEMS

Evolutionary algorithms are a class of optimization algorithms inspired by the processes of natural selection and biological evolution to solve complex problems. These algorithms seek optimal or near-optimal solutions by simulating the fundamental mechanisms of biological evolution, such as reproduction, mutation, selection, and crossover (genetic recombination). One of the most well-known evolutionary algorithms is the genetic algorithm, which mimics the way organisms evolve and adapt over time.

Evolutionary algorithms are particularly useful for solving optimization and search problems in large solution spaces, where traditional computational techniques may fail or become too costly in terms of time and resources.

How Do Evolutionary Algorithms Work?

Evolutionary algorithms operate on a population of candidate solutions to a given problem. These initial solutions are often generated randomly and represent the starting point on which the algorithm will work. During the execution of the algorithm, each solution is evaluated using a fitness function, which measures how close the solution is to a desired or optimal result.

The basic cycle of an evolutionary algorithm follows these steps:

1. Initialization: A population of initial solutions is created, often randomly. Each individual in the population represents a possible solution to the problem.

2. Evaluation (Fitness): Each solution is evaluated using a fitness function. This function assigns a score to the solution, indicating how "good" it is relative to the problem being solved. For example, if the goal is to optimize the design of an airplane, the fitness function might measure aerodynamic efficiency or fuel consumption.

3. Selection: The best solutions, those with the highest fitness scores, are selected to move on to the next phase. The idea is that better solutions have a higher probability of reproducing, similar to natural selection.

4. Reproduction (Crossover): The selected solutions combine with each other (similar to biological reproduction) to create new solutions. This process of genetic recombination or crossover allows the mixing of the best features of the selected solutions to form new individuals.

5. Mutation: To prevent the algorithm from getting stuck in suboptimal solutions, a mutation mechanism is introduced. This mechanism randomly alters parts of the solutions, introducing variations that could lead to improvements or discoveries of new, more effective solutions.

6. Iteration: The steps of evaluation, selection, reproduction, and mutation are repeated for many generations. Each new generation should, in theory, get closer and closer to the optimal solution of the problem.

Practical Example: Optimizing Aircraft Design with Genetic Algorithms

A successful practical application of evolutionary algorithms, especially genetic algorithms, is in optimizing aircraft design. Aerodynamic design is a complex problem that requires balancing many variables, such as air resistance, weight, fuel consumption, and stability. Traditional optimization methods, such as those based on analytical calculations or engineering simulations, can be slow and expensive.

Here's how a genetic algorithm can be used to optimize the design of an aircraft:

1. Problem Representation: Each possible aircraft design is represented as a "genetic string" composed of various parameters, such as wing shape, angle of incidence, and aspect ratio. Each parameter is encoded as a sequence of numbers or discrete values.

2. Fitness Function: A fitness function is defined to evaluate the effectiveness of the design. This function may take into account various factors, such as fuel consumption, maximum speed, stability, and payload capacity. For example, a design that reduces air resistance without compromising stability would receive a higher fitness score.

3. Selection and Recombination: Designs with the highest fitness scores are selected for reproduction. They are combined to create new designs, mixing the best features of both "parents." For example, an aerodynamic wing shape from one parent might be combined with a lightweight fuselage from another.

4. Mutation: A random mutation is applied to certain parts of the design, such as wing length or angle of attack. This introduces variations that may lead to even more effective designs.

5. Simulations: The new designs are tested in aerodynamic simulations, such as virtual wind tunnels, to determine their effectiveness.

6. Ongoing Evolution: After several generations, the evolutionary process produces increasingly efficient designs. The final result is an optimized aircraft capable of meeting the required performance standards.

This genetic algorithm-based approach is used by aerospace and engineering companies to explore vast design spaces that would be impractical to explore manually. It is also widely used in the automotive industry, wind turbine design, and other sectors that require the complex optimization of multiple variables.

Advantages and Limitations of Evolutionary Algorithms

Evolutionary algorithms offer many advantages:

- Flexibility: They can be applied to a wide range of problems, from mathematical to engineering challenges.

- Global Search: They are highly effective in finding global solutions rather than getting stuck in local suboptimal solutions, thanks to the mutation mechanism.

- No Preliminary Knowledge Required: Detailed knowledge of the problem is not necessary; the algorithm autonomously explores the solutions.

However, evolutionary algorithms also have some limitations:

- High Computational Costs: Due to their iterative nature, they can take a long time and require substantial resources to converge on an optimal solution.

- No Guarantee of Optimal Solutions: While they tend to improve over time, there is no guarantee that they will always find the optimal solution.

Evolutionary algorithms, particularly genetic algorithms, represent a powerful tool for solving complex optimization problems across a wide range of fields, from aerospace to engineering. Thanks to their biological inspiration, they are able to explore vast and dynamic solution spaces, often producing results that surpass those obtained with traditional methods. In the next chapter, we will explore other advanced artificial intelligence techniques and how they integrate to solve real-world challenges.

CHAPTER 4: Deep Learning: Advanced Architectures

CONVOLUTIONAL NEURAL NETWORKS (CNN)

Convolutional Neural Networks (CNN) are among the most powerful and widely used tools in deep learning, especially when it comes to recognizing images or objects in photos. CNNs are designed to process data with a grid-like structure, such as images, where pixels are organized in rows and columns. Unlike traditional neural networks, which treat each input independently, CNNs exploit the spatial correlation between data. This means they can capture the local features of images, such as edges, textures, and shapes, to recognize complex objects in a visual context.

Basic Structure of CNNs

Convolutional neural networks are distinguished by their architecture, which is composed of three main types of layers: convolutional layers, pooling layers, and fully connected layers.

1. Convolutional Layer: This is the core of a CNN. In the convolutional layer, a series of filters (also called kernels) are slid over the image. Each filter is a small matrix that detects specific features such as edges, corners, or textures. The result of this operation is called an activation map, which highlights the areas of the image where a particular feature is present. The more convolutional layers are used, the more detailed and complex the detected features become.

2. Pooling Layer: After one or more convolutional layers, a pooling layer is applied, usually max-pooling. This layer reduces the spatial size of the

image while keeping the most relevant information. For instance, max-pooling takes the maximum value within a small region of the activation map. This has two main advantages: it reduces the number of parameters to process and makes the model more robust to variations in the object's position within the image.

3. Fully Connected Layer: Towards the end of the network, after several convolutional and pooling layers, CNNs include one or more fully connected layers. At this stage, all the information processed in the previous steps is combined to generate a final prediction. This layer works similarly to traditional neural networks, where each neuron is connected to all the neurons in the previous layer.

Practical Example: Classifying Animal Images

A common example of using CNNs is image classification. Suppose we want to train a convolutional neural network to distinguish between images of cats, dogs, and other animals.

1. Input: The animal images are provided as input to the network, and each image is represented as a grid of pixels. Each pixel has a numerical value indicating the color and light intensity.

2. Convolution: In the convolutional layer, filters scan the image to find distinctive elements. One filter might detect the edge of an ear, while another might highlight a dog's snout. The more convolutional layers are used, the more the network learns to recognize increasingly complex features.

3. Pooling: Each time pooling is applied, the image size is reduced, but the network retains essential information. For example, even if the original image of a dog is reduced, the network still preserves the fundamental features, such as the general shape of the snout or the position of the ears.

4. Final Prediction: After processing, the image passes through the fully connected layers. The network combines all the learned information to make a prediction. In the end, the output could be a probability associated with each category: for instance, the image has an 85% chance of being a dog, 10% a cat, and 5% a horse.

Advantages of CNNs

CNNs offer several advantages over traditional neural networks:

1. Parameter Reduction: Thanks to the use of filters, CNNs have fewer parameters to train compared to fully connected networks. This makes them more efficient, especially with large images.

2. Spatial Invariance: CNNs are particularly suited to recognizing objects in different positions, scales, and orientations within images. This means that even if the object shifts within the image, the network will still be able to identify it correctly.

3. Adaptability: CNNs are used not only for image classification but also for a variety of tasks related to computer vision, such as facial recognition, medical image segmentation, and real-time object detection.

Convolutional Neural Networks (CNN) represent one of the most advanced architectures in deep learning, designed to solve complex computer vision problems. By utilizing convolutional filters and pooling layers, CNNs can efficiently analyze images, identifying objects and recognizing patterns even in complex situations. Their ability to reduce the number of parameters while maintaining accuracy makes them a powerful tool for numerous applications in artificial intelligence.

RECURRENT NEURAL NETWORKS (RNNs)

Recurrent Neural Networks (RNNs) are a specific type of neural network designed to process sequential data, where the order of the inputs matters. They are used in fields like Natural Language Processing (NLP), time series analysis, and other applications where there is a temporal dependency between the data. This makes them ideal for tasks such as machine translation, stock market prediction, speech recognition, and text analysis.

Structure of RNNs

Unlike traditional neural networks, where neurons work in parallel and independently, RNNs are designed to retain a memory of previous information through the use of recursive loops. This means that each neuron not only considers its current input but also the one from the previous step. In other words, there is a cyclic connection that allows the network to "remember" what it has seen before.

The key element that distinguishes RNNs from other architectures is the presence of a "memory tape," which allows them to handle input sequences of variable length and preserve the temporal context of the data.

How RNNs Work

The main mechanism of an RNN is as follows:

1. Sequential Input: RNNs process a sequence of data one step at a time. Each step in the sequence is passed to the network, and the information is processed while taking previous inputs into account.

2. Recurrent Connections: At each step, the output of the neuron is sent to the next step and "recycled" through a recurrent connection. This way, the network can accumulate and remember information about all previous steps.

3. Prediction: At the end of the sequence, the network produces an output, which could be a translation into another language, a prediction of a future value in a time series, or the recognition of a word or phrase.

Challenges with RNNs: Vanishing Gradients

Despite their usefulness, RNNs have some limitations. A common issue is the "vanishing gradients" problem, which makes it difficult to train RNNs on long sequences. This occurs because, as the network processes more steps in the sequence, information from the early stages can be lost, reducing the network's ability to handle long-term dependencies.

To address this issue, variants of RNNs have been developed, such as LSTMs (Long Short-Term Memory) and GRUs (Gated Recurrent Units), which better preserve long-term information.

Practical Examples of RNNs

1. Machine Translation A common example of RNN use is in machine translation of text from one language to another, as seen in Google Translate. When you input a sentence in one language, the recurrent neural network analyzes the sentence word by word, keeping track of previous words to maintain context. This is crucial because the meaning of a word in a sentence often depends on the words that precede it. For instance, in English, the word "bank" can refer to a financial institution or the side of a river, depending on the context. The ability of RNNs to track previous words helps them translate complex sentences more accurately.

Here's how it works:

- The RNN processes one word at a time.

- It uses the context of previous words to understand the meaning of the sentence.

- At the end of the sequence, the network produces the translated sentence in the target language.

2. Stock Market Prediction Time series are another field where RNNs excel. A practical example is stock price prediction. RNNs can be trained

on historical market data to predict future stock prices based on past patterns.

Here's how it works in this context:

- The network analyzes historical stock price data day by day (or hourly).

- At each step, the RNN uses information from the previous day to make a prediction for the next day.

- This process enables more accurate predictions, as the network "remembers" how prices behaved in the recent past.

Advantages of RNNs

- Sequential Memory: RNNs can retain memory of previous inputs, making them ideal for tasks where the order of data is important, such as text or speech.

- Processing of Variable-Length Sequences: They can handle input sequences of varying lengths, making them highly flexible.

- Real-Time Applications: RNNs can be used for real-time applications, such as chatbots or voice recognition systems.

Recurrent Neural Networks (RNNs) are essential for processing sequential data, where the order of inputs is critical. By using cyclic connections, these networks can "remember" previous information to improve future predictions. This makes them particularly suited for tasks like machine translation, where word context is crucial, and stock market prediction, where the network must track past trends. Despite their limitations with long sequences, variants like LSTM and GRU have significantly improved their performance, making them a powerful tool in the world of deep learning.

TRANSFORMERS AND LANGUAGE MODELS

Transformers are one of the most revolutionary and advanced architectures in Natural Language Processing (NLP). Introduced in 2017 with the famous paper "Attention is All You Need", transformers quickly supplanted Recurrent Neural Networks (RNNs) and other traditional architectures due to their ability to handle text sequences more efficiently and accurately. Unlike RNNs, which process data sequentially, transformers use a mechanism called self-attention, allowing them to process all elements of a sequence simultaneously while maintaining a global view of the context.

One of the most well-known examples of a transformer-based model is GPT-3 (Generative Pretrained Transformer 3), which has demonstrated extraordinary writing and automatic text generation capabilities, making this technology a milestone in the field of artificial intelligence.

Structure of Transformers

Transformers rely primarily on an attention mechanism and consist of two main components:

1. Encoder: The encoder takes the input (for example, a sentence) and transforms it into a numerical representation that captures the

meaning of the words and the relationships between them. Encoders apply self-attention, allowing the network to "pay more attention" to certain words in the sentence that are more relevant to the context. For example, in a sentence like "The dog chased the cat," the model will recognize that "dog" and "cat" are important and related words.

2. Decoder: The decoder uses the representations created by the encoder to generate an output. This is particularly useful for tasks like text generation, such as machine translation or sentence writing, as the decoder can use the context provided by the encoder to generate a coherent and well-structured sequence of text.

Self-Attention Mechanism

Self-attention is the core of the transformer. This mechanism allows the model to assign different "weights" to each word in a sentence in relation to all the other words, considering not just nearby words but all the words in the sequence at once. This is what distinguishes transformers from RNNs, which process one word at a time, making it difficult to retain long-term memory.

Thanks to self-attention, transformers can capture long-term relationships and complex interactions between words in a sequence, making them ideal for tasks such as machine translation, text summarization, or answering complex questions automatically.

Practical Example: GPT-3 and Automatic Writing of Complex Texts

GPT-3 (Generative Pretrained Transformer 3) is one of the most advanced examples of a transformer-based model. It has been trained on a vast corpus of texts covering virtually every imaginable topic, and it can generate high-quality text that often appears indistinguishable from that written by a human.

GPT-3 operates on a simple yet powerful principle: it is provided with a prompt or initial text input, and the model completes the text by generating new sentences that are consistent with what has already been written. For example, if you give GPT-3 a sentence like "Once there was a small village at the foot of a mountain," the model will continue to develop the story, adding details and creating a full narrative while maintaining the storyline and context.

How GPT-3 works in practice:

1. Input: The user provides a text input, which can be a question, an initial piece of information, or a writing prompt.

2. Processing: The model analyzes the provided text and uses the billions of parameters it has been trained on to determine the most likely next words, based on the context of the prompt and the linguistic patterns it learned during training.

3. Output: GPT-3 generates a response or continuation of the text, which can range from a single sentence to entire paragraphs. The model is capable of writing articles, answering complex questions, generating code, and even creating creative texts, such as poems or stories.

Examples of GPT-3 use cases:

- Creative writing: GPT-3 is used to help writers and journalists generate ideas or draft articles.

- Virtual assistants: It is employed to create more natural automatic responses in chatbots and virtual assistants.

- Code generation: GPT-3 can write source code in various programming languages based on natural language descriptions.

Advantages of Transformers

- Efficiency: Transformers can process data in parallel, making them much more efficient than RNNs, which have to process data sequentially.

- Contextual Understanding: Thanks to the self-attention mechanism, transformers can understand complex relationships between words, even at a distance, improving performance in NLP tasks.

- Flexibility: Transformers can be used in a wide range of applications, from machine translation to content generation, text classification, and much more.

Transformers have revolutionized the field of Natural Language Processing by introducing a more efficient and effective way of processing complex texts. Thanks to the self-attention mechanism, these networks can manage relationships between distant words in a text, greatly improving the capabilities of models like GPT-3, which has demonstrated how powerful they can be in generating complex and realistic texts. With the advancement of transformer-based models, the possibilities for linguistic and creative applications continue to expand.

AUTOENCODERS AND VARIATIONAL NETWORKS

Autoencoders and variational neural networks are powerful techniques in deep learning, primarily used for data compression and the generation of new data. These are neural networks designed to learn a compact representation (or encoding) of input data, capable of compressing and then reconstructing information by eliminating irrelevant details. Specifically, variational autoencoders (VAEs) are an advanced variant of autoencoders and are used to generate realistic new data, such as human faces or images of objects.

These techniques find application in various fields, such as image noise reduction, data compression, and the generation of synthetic content, including images or videos.

How Autoencoders Work

Autoencoders are neural networks designed to learn a reduced representation of the input. The architecture of an autoencoder is divided into two main parts:

1. Encoder: The encoder takes the original input (e.g., an image) and transforms it into a more compact representation, called a code or latent space. This latent space is a simplified version of the data that contains the most important features of the input.

2. Decoder: The decoder takes this compact representation and converts it back into the original format. The goal is for the final output of the decoder to be as similar as possible to the original input.

The key idea is that the autoencoder learns to compress data by retaining relevant information and discarding superfluous details. This ability to learn a compact representation makes autoencoders useful for data compression and the dimensionality reduction of complex datasets.

Example: Image Noise Reduction

A practical application of autoencoders is image noise reduction. Often, when taking a photo in low light conditions or with a low-quality camera, visual noise is introduced that degrades the image. Autoencoders can be trained to clean these images by removing noise and improving quality.

Here's how it works:

- Input: A noisy image is provided as input to the autoencoder.

- Encoder: The encoder compresses the image, eliminating noise or other irrelevant information.

- Decoder: The decoder reconstructs the clean image, retaining the essential features but without the noise.

During training, the autoencoder learns to recognize the distinctive features of the original image and separate them from the noise, resulting in a cleaner, sharper image.

Variational Networks (VAEs)

Variational autoencoders (VAEs) are a more sophisticated version of traditional autoencoders. In addition to compressing data, VAEs are designed to generate new realistic data that follows a probabilistic distribution similar to the original data. Instead of learning a fixed representation of the data like traditional autoencoders, VAEs learn a probabilistic representation.

The operation of VAEs is based on the idea of transforming the input into a statistical distribution rather than a single point in latent space. The latent space of a VAE is not a single encoding but a distribution from which new points can be sampled. This feature allows VAEs to generate new realistic examples that are not part of the original dataset but appear very similar to the training data.

Example: Generating Realistic Faces

One of the most fascinating uses of VAEs is generating realistic human faces. After being trained on a large dataset of human face images, VAEs can be used to generate synthetic faces that look incredibly realistic but do not belong to any real person.

Here's how it works:

1. Training: The VAE is trained on thousands of images of real faces. The encoder learns to compress each face into a distribution of points in latent space, while the decoder learns to reconstruct the face from this distribution.

2. Generating New Faces: Once trained, the VAE can sample new random points in latent space. These points, once passed through the decoder, are transformed into completely new faces that do not exist in the original dataset.

3. Variability: By slightly modifying the values within the latent space, variations of a specific face can be generated. For example, the same face can be rendered with different expressions or angles without requiring new input.

Practical Applications of Autoencoders and VAEs

1. Data Compression: Autoencoders can be used to reduce the size of complex data, such as images or audio signals, without losing key information. This compression can be useful for reducing storage requirements or speeding up data transmission over networks.

2. Content Generation: VAEs are used to create synthetic content, such as images, videos, or audio. They can be employed to generate new virtual reality scenarios, design 3D objects, or even create music.

3. Anomaly Detection: Autoencoders are also used for anomaly detection. Since an autoencoder learns to reconstruct "normal" data, any anomalous or out-of-the-ordinary data will be reconstructed with significant error. This is useful, for instance, in detecting faults in machinery or uncovering financial fraud.

Autoencoders and VAEs are powerful deep learning tools with a wide range of applications, from data compression to the generation of new content. While traditional autoencoders focus on dimensionality reduction and faithful data reconstruction, VAEs introduce the ability to generate new data that follows the same statistical rules as the training dataset, opening new possibilities for creating synthetic content and simulation.

GENERATIVE ADVERSARIAL NETWORKS (GANs)

Generative Adversarial Networks (GANs) are one of the most innovative and fascinating techniques in deep learning, particularly known for their ability to create realistic images, videos, and other content that does not exist in reality. GANs are used in a wide range of creative and technical applications, from generative design to the creation of synthetic data to improve AI models.

The concept behind GANs was introduced in 2014 by Ian Goodfellow, and their power lies in the innovative approach they use: two neural networks, called the generator and the discriminator, compete against each other in a kind of zero-sum game. This "competitive" dynamic is what allows GANs to generate high-quality content.

How GANs Work

GANs consist of two distinct neural networks that work together:

1. Generator: The generator is responsible for creating new data, such as images, from random input. Its goal is to generate content so realistic that it fools the discriminator, which is the second network.

2. Discriminator: The discriminator is trained to distinguish between real data (from the training dataset) and fake data (generated by the generator). Its job is to determine whether an image is authentic or generated.

The dynamic works as follows: the generator creates an image from random noise, trying to fool the discriminator. The discriminator analyzes the image and decides whether it is real or fake. If the discriminator recognizes that it's fake, the generator learns from its mistakes and improves the image quality in the next iteration. Over time, the generator becomes increasingly skilled at creating realistic images, while the discriminator becomes better at distinguishing them, in a process of mutual improvement.

Practical Example: Creating Realistic Human Faces

One of the most well-known uses of GANs is the creation of realistic human face images that do not exist in reality. This has been popularized by projects like "This Person Does Not Exist", where each time you visit the website, a completely new and realistic face of a non-existent person is generated.

Here's how it works:

1. Training: The generator is trained on a massive dataset of real faces, such as the famous CelebA dataset, which contains thousands of celebrity photos. During training, the generator attempts to create human faces from random noise, while the discriminator learns to recognize real faces from generated ones.

2. Progressive Improvement: At the start of the process, the generator produces faces that are easily recognizable as fake (they may have distorted or unrealistic features). However, as time and iterations go by, the generator learns to produce increasingly realistic faces, refining details such as eye shape, skin color, and facial expressions, eventually creating images that are almost indistinguishable from real photographs.

3. Final Output: After many training iterations, the generator becomes skilled enough to create realistic faces that can even fool humans. Each time a new face is requested, the generator uses the accumulated learning to produce a completely new image, different from any real face in the dataset.

Applications of GANs

GANs have enormous potential across various fields, especially in content generation and the synthesis of realistic data. Here are some of their most important applications:

1. Generation of Realistic Images and Videos: GANs can generate not only static images like faces or landscapes but also realistic videos. This can be used to create virtual scenes for films or video games, reducing the need for expensive special effects.

2. Data Augmentation: In many situations, obtaining sufficient data to train an AI model can be difficult. GANs can generate synthetic data to expand an existing dataset. For example, they can create synthetic medical images to train diagnostic models or images for autonomous driving systems to improve self-driving cars.

3. Image Restoration: GANs are used for restoring damaged or low-quality images. They can restore old photographs or improve the resolution of blurry images, such as in super-resolution processes, where a low-resolution image is converted into a high-resolution one.

4. Creation of Artworks: GANs are also used to create generative art. They can take an artistic style (such as Van Gogh's or Monet's) and apply it to images or videos, creating unique and original works.

Challenges and Limitations of GANs

Despite their power, GANs have some challenges and limitations. One major issue is mode collapse, where the generator starts producing the same type of output repeatedly, ignoring the variety in input data. Additionally, GANs require very long and complex training, and finding a balance between the generator and discriminator is difficult; if one becomes too strong compared to the other, the system can stop working properly.

Generative Adversarial Networks (GANs) are a crucial innovation in deep learning, opening new possibilities for creating realistic images and videos and synthesizing data. Through the competitive dynamic between the generator and discriminator, GANs can create incredibly realistic content, such as human faces that do not exist in reality. Thanks to GANs, applications ranging from creative design to data science are reaching new levels of sophistication and power.

DIFFERENCES BETWEEN MACHINE LEARNING AND DEEP LEARNING

While both machine learning and deep learning are systems used in artificial intelligence (AI) to train models and prepare algorithms for specific tasks, the main difference lies in the complexity of the techniques used and the types of problems these techniques can solve. Both are part of AI, but deep learning is a sub-category of machine learning:

1. Complexity and Capability

Traditional machine learning relies on simpler algorithms and requires manual feature selection for analysis. It is suited for less complex problems and does not necessarily require large amounts of data.

Deep learning, through deep neural networks, can handle much more complex problems, such as natural language understanding or computer vision. However, it requires vast amounts of data and significant computational power.

2. Feature Extraction

In machine learning, relevant features must be manually selected by engineers (feature engineering).

In deep learning, neural networks autonomously learn which features are important from raw data.

3. Data and Computational Power

Traditional machine learning works well with small datasets and requires less computational power.

Deep learning requires enormous amounts of data to achieve high performance and leverages advanced hardware such as GPUs and TPUs.

4. Applications

Machine learning is used in applications like spam email filtering, price prediction, medical diagnosis, and other tasks that can be solved with structured datasets.

Deep learning excels in applications that require the understanding of complex patterns, such as image recognition, autonomous driving, speech recognition, and machine translation.

Practical Example: Image Recognition (Dogs vs. Cats)

1. Approach with Traditional Machine Learning

In traditional machine learning, to solve the problem of recognizing images of dogs and cats, the following steps are taken:

Data Collection: Obtain a labeled dataset of images where each image is associated with its correct category ("dog" or "cat").

Feature Extraction: This is one of the most important steps in traditional machine learning. Instead of using the "raw" images directly, relevant features must be manually extracted. An engineer might, for example, identify:

Geometric features: The shape of the ears or snout.

Texture: Whether the fur is smooth or rough.

Color: The distribution of colors in the image.

Engineers may use tools to extract these features or write specific algorithms for this purpose. The model works only on these extracted features, not the entire image.

Model Training: Classical machine learning algorithms are used, such as:

SVM (Support Vector Machine)

Decision Trees

K-Nearest Neighbors (KNN)

The model is trained on this transformed data (the extracted features) to learn to distinguish between dogs and cats.

Prediction: Once trained, the model receives a new image, performs the same feature extraction, and makes a prediction based on the identified features.

Advantages and Disadvantages:

Advantage: Works well on small datasets and doesn't require extremely powerful hardware.

Disadvantage: Accuracy heavily depends on the quality of the feature selection, which requires specific knowledge and manual intervention.

2. Approach with Deep Learning (Convolutional Neural Networks - CNN)

In deep learning, you can use a Convolutional Neural Network (CNN) to solve the same problem, but the process is more automated:

Data Collection: As with traditional machine learning, you collect a labeled dataset of images, with "dog" and "cat" categories.

Training with the CNN:

Instead of manually extracting features, the CNN works directly on raw images.

The CNN has layers that automatically identify patterns in the image. Initially, the network recognizes simple features, like edges and shapes, and then deeper layers detect more complex structures, such as the overall shape of a dog's or cat's face.

CNN Architecture:

Convolutional Layer: Detects features like edges and textures.

Pooling Layer: Reduces the size of the identified features to make the model more efficient.

Fully Connected Layer: In the end, the network combines all the identified features to make the final prediction: "dog" or "cat."

Prediction: After training, the CNN receives a new image and makes a prediction based on the automatic analysis of patterns learned during training.

Advantages and Disadvantages:

Advantage: The CNN can automatically learn from images, without the need to manually extract features. It also achieves higher accuracy, especially on complex problems and very large datasets.

Disadvantage: It requires a large amount of data to obtain good results and significant computational power (GPU) to train the model.

This concludes Chapters 3 and 4, where we covered two fundamental technical topics: machine learning and deep learning. Though complex, they are the foundation of artificial intelligence, so it was essential to address them carefully. I've tried to explain these concepts as clearly as possible, using practical examples and brief summaries at the end of each point to help you better understand.

Now that we've finished the more technical parts, we can relax a bit! In the next chapters, we'll dive into other AI-related topics, which will be more application-focused and less "mathematical." Ready to continue? You just need to turn the page... literally.

CHAPTER 5: Applications of Artificial Intelligence in Industrial Sectors

In this chapter, we will explore the numerous practical applications of artificial intelligence across various industrial sectors, demonstrating how AI is transforming the world of work and production processes. From healthcare to finance, from logistics to manufacturing, we will see how these technologies are improving efficiency, optimizing resources, and enabling innovations once considered unimaginable. Through concrete examples, this chapter will give you a clear overview of how AI is already being used today to solve real-world problems and create new opportunities in key economic sectors.

HEALTHCARE: DIAGNOSIS AND PERSONALIZED TREATMENTS

Artificial intelligence (AI) is rapidly transforming the healthcare sector, revolutionizing how doctors diagnose diseases and personalize treatments for patients. Thanks to advanced techniques like machine learning and deep learning (have you heard of them?), AI systems can analyze vast amounts of medical data, identify patterns invisible to the human eye, and provide more accurate and personalized diagnoses and treatment plans. This leads to faster diagnoses, tailored treatments, and, in many cases, better patient outcomes.

Medical Diagnosis with AI

One of the most promising uses of AI in healthcare is the automatic diagnosis of diseases through the analysis of medical images. AI tools, particularly

Convolutional Neural Networks (CNNs), are trained to recognize specific patterns in images such as X-rays, MRIs, CT scans, and mammograms. These tools can detect anomalies and signs of diseases with a very high level of accuracy, often comparable to or even surpassing that of a human radiologist.

Example: Breast Cancer Detection

A concrete example is the use of neural networks for detecting breast cancer in mammograms. Deep learning algorithms are trained on large datasets of images, some of which show tumors and some that do not. These models can "learn" to recognize the signs of cancer, such as the presence of microcalcifications or suspicious masses, even in the early stages of the disease. With AI, doctors can achieve more accurate diagnoses, reducing the number of false positives and false negatives.

The ability of CNNs to analyze complex images and detect diseases early is significantly improving patient survival rates, allowing doctors to intervene earlier and more precisely.

Personalized Treatments with AI

Beyond diagnosis, AI is opening new frontiers in the creation of personalized treatments, also known as precision medicine. Traditionally, treatments are prescribed based on general guidelines that may not take into account the unique characteristics of each patient. However, AI can analyze patients' genetic, clinical, and environmental data to create personalized therapies.

Example: Personalized Oncology

In oncology, AI is used to analyze the genetic profile of both the patient and the tumor. For example, there are different types of lung cancer, each of which responds differently to treatments. By analyzing the tumor's DNA and combining it with patient data, AI can recommend the most effective treatment for that particular patient, reducing the risk of unnecessary side effects and improving the chances of success.

This approach allows doctors to move away from the traditional "one-size-fits-all" treatment method and propose more targeted and potentially more effective therapies. In oncology, AI is also used to predict how a patient will respond to a specific drug, assessing the risk of treatment resistance or relapse.

Continuous Monitoring and Prevention

AI is not limited to diagnoses and treatments; it is also used for the continuous monitoring of patients, particularly those with chronic diseases, and for prevention. Wearable devices like smartwatches or biometric sensors collect real-time health data, such as heart rate, blood pressure, oxygen levels, and other vital signs. AI analyzes these data in real-time, identifying patterns that may indicate an emerging medical condition, such as a heart attack or hyperglycemic episode.

For example, in diabetic patients, AI can monitor glucose levels and provide personalized recommendations for diet or insulin administration, preventing severe complications. This type of intelligent monitoring reduces the need for frequent medical visits and helps patients manage their condition more effectively.

Challenges and Opportunities

Despite the great progress, there are still some challenges to overcome in the use of AI in healthcare. One of the main issues is the need for high-quality data. AI depends on access to large quantities of accurate and diverse data to provide reliable predictions, and not all hospitals or healthcare systems have such data available. Additionally, there are concerns about data privacy and security, as healthcare information is highly sensitive.

However, the opportunities presented by AI are immense. The automation of diagnoses and the personalization of treatments are leading to more efficient and personalized medicine, offering better care at lower costs. As technology continues to evolve and improve, AI is expected to have an even greater impact on improving care quality and managing complex or chronic diseases.

In summary, AI is radically changing the healthcare sector, from rapid and accurate diagnoses to the creation of personalized treatments based on genetic and clinical data. Thanks to its ability to analyze large volumes of data, artificial intelligence is helping to improve clinical outcomes, providing healthcare that is more precise, proactive, and tailored to patients' specific needs.

FINANCE: ALGORITHMIC TRADING AND RISK ANALYSIS

Artificial intelligence (AI) is profoundly transforming the financial sector, with applications ranging from algorithmic trading to risk analysis and fraud detection. By using advanced machine learning algorithms, financial institutions can make faster decisions, optimize strategies, and prevent illicit activities. AI has become an indispensable tool for improving efficiency and security in financial markets, helping investors make more informed decisions and preventing significant losses.

Algorithmic Trading

One of the most well-known uses of AI in finance is algorithmic trading, or algo-trading, which involves the use of algorithms to execute trades automatically and quickly. In this context, machine learning is used to analyze large amounts of historical and real-time data, searching for patterns and trends in the markets that can be exploited to make profitable trades.

How Does Algorithmic Trading Work?

In algorithmic trading, algorithms are designed to follow a set of predefined rules for buying or selling financial assets such as stocks, bonds, or currencies. These algorithms analyze various factors, such as market prices, trading volumes, technical indicators, and even real-time news. Once a favorable pattern is identified, the system automatically executes the trade within milliseconds, taking advantage of opportunities that would be impossible for a human trader to capture due to the speed required.

Practical Example: Predicting Market Fluctuations

Machine learning algorithms can be trained on historical data to predict market fluctuations. For instance, an algorithm might analyze years of data on a specific stock and identify how certain factors, such as interest rate changes or shifts in trading volumes, impact its price. Using this information, the algorithm can make predictions about the stock's future behavior and recommend buy or sell operations.

Additionally, AI can analyze market sentiment through natural language processing (NLP) techniques, examining news articles, social media posts, and other sources to understand investor sentiment. For example, a surge in positive discussions about a particular company could lead to a rise in its stock price, and the algorithm can anticipate these trends in real-time, helping investors make more informed decisions.

Risk Analysis and Fraud Detection

Another area where AI is essential is in risk analysis and fraud detection. Banks and financial institutions are constantly exposed to risks, such as credit risk, market risk, or operational risk, and AI can help manage them more effectively.

Machine Learning for Risk Analysis

Machine learning techniques can analyze vast amounts of financial data to identify risk factors and predict potential problems. For example, in banking, algorithms can be used to analyze customer behavior and determine their likelihood of default (i.e., the probability that a customer will not repay a loan). By analyzing data such as income, credit history, age, and job stability, AI can accurately calculate the risk associated with a loan and help banks make more informed decisions about granting credit.

Practical Example: Fraud Detection

Fraud detection is another critical area where AI is making significant progress. Traditional fraud detection methods often rely on fixed rules, such as automatically blocking transactions above a certain amount in high-risk regions. However, these systems can be too rigid, generating many false positives (unnecessary blocks) or failing to detect more subtle fraudulent activities.

Machine learning, on the other hand, can analyze each user's behavior in real-time and recognize anomalous patterns that might indicate fraud. For example, if a user suddenly starts making unusual purchases or transferring money in ways inconsistent with their past behavior, the algorithm could flag it as suspicious. A machine learning algorithm could also detect complex fraud schemes, such as fraud distributed across multiple accounts or transactions carried out using stolen identities.

Moreover, AI can learn from new data and adapt to emerging fraud patterns, making the detection system more dynamic and accurate compared to traditional methods. This reduces the risk for financial institutions and helps better protect customers from unjustified losses.

Advantages of AI in Finance

The use of AI in areas such as algorithmic trading and risk analysis offers numerous advantages:

1. Speed: AI algorithms can execute trades and analyses in a fraction of a second, seizing opportunities that would be missed by human traders.

2. Accuracy: AI can reduce human error and improve the accuracy of predictions, lowering risks.

3. Adaptability: Machine learning algorithms can adapt to new data and change strategies in real-time, continuously improving their performance.

Artificial intelligence has revolutionized the world of finance, with practical applications ranging from algorithmic trading to risk analysis and fraud detection. Thanks to the use of machine learning, financial institutions can make faster and more informed decisions, improving profitability and transaction security. With the continued advancement of technology, the role of AI in finance will only expand, offering more opportunities to optimize processes and enhance risk management.

MANUFACTURING AND LOGISTICS

Artificial intelligence (AI) is radically transforming the manufacturing and logistics sectors, improving efficiency, reducing costs, and increasing productivity. Through advanced techniques such as machine learning, robotics, and predictive analytics, companies can automate processes, optimize supply chains, and intelligently manage daily operations. AI also enables demand forecasting and proactive responses to market changes, enhancing companies' agility in an increasingly competitive world.

Supply Chain Optimization

One of the areas where AI is having a significant impact is supply chain optimization. Companies must manage complex flows of goods and materials across various suppliers, warehouses, and distributors. AI improves the management of these processes through data analysis and forecasting future needs.

Example: Demand Forecasting

With machine learning algorithms, companies can analyze historical sales data, seasonal factors, market trends, and even unexpected events to predict future demand. These predictive models help businesses optimize raw material orders and reduce storage costs. For example, an automobile manufacturer can analyze past sales data and consumer trends to determine how many components will be needed in the coming months, avoiding both overstocking and shortages that could slow down production.

Moreover, AI can monitor real-time fluctuations in the supply chain, such as supplier delays or changes in material prices, and suggest immediate adjustments, such as sourcing alternative suppliers or modifying transportation routes.

Example: Logistics Optimization

AI also plays a crucial role in logistics optimization. AI algorithms can calculate the most efficient routes for transporting goods by considering factors such as traffic, weather conditions, fuel consumption, and vehicle capacity. This leads to reduced transportation costs, more timely deliveries, and lower CO_2 emissions.

A concrete example is the use of AI-powered fleet management systems, which track the location of trucks, optimize routes, and plan preventive maintenance for vehicles to avoid unexpected breakdowns. Amazon, for instance, uses these systems to ensure fast and efficient deliveries on a large scale.

Automation of Production Processes

In the manufacturing sector, AI underpins many advanced technologies that are changing how products are made. One of the most significant applications is the use of intelligent robots, which are automating numerous production processes, increasing precision, and reducing production times.

Example: Intelligent Robots in Factories

AI-powered industrial robots can perform repetitive tasks but also adapt to changes in the work environment, making them much more versatile than traditional robots. For example, in automotive assembly lines, intelligent robots can perform assembly and welding operations with millimeter precision while continuously learning from the tasks they perform, improving over time through machine learning.

These robots can also work in collaboration with human workers, creating hybrid production systems where robots handle the most dangerous or physically demanding tasks, while workers focus on supervision and quality control. This improves workplace safety and the quality of finished products.

Example: Predictive Maintenance

Another crucial application of AI in manufacturing is predictive maintenance. Sensors installed on machinery collect real-time data on performance, such as temperature, vibrations, and energy consumption. AI algorithms analyze this data to predict when a machine might fail, allowing maintenance to be performed before production interruptions occur. This approach reduces unplanned downtime and repair costs, improving the overall efficiency of the factory.

Benefits of AI in Manufacturing and Logistics

Integrating artificial intelligence into manufacturing and logistics processes offers numerous benefits:

1. Reduced Operating Costs: Process automation and transportation route optimization reduce overall costs.

2. Increased Efficiency: Demand forecasting and predictive maintenance improve resource management and reduce downtime.

3. Greater Precision: The use of intelligent robots enhances the precision of production processes, reducing human errors.

Artificial intelligence is revolutionizing the manufacturing and logistics sectors, enabling companies to be more agile and competitive. From supply chain optimization to predictive maintenance and the use of intelligent robots, AI is transforming industrial processes, reducing costs, improving quality, and making the entire production chain more efficient. As technology continues to advance, AI will drive innovations that define the future of manufacturing and logistics.

PRECISION AGRICULTURE

Precision agriculture is an innovative approach that leverages artificial intelligence (AI) and other advanced technologies to improve the efficiency and sustainability of farming activities. The goal is to optimize the use of resources such as water, fertilizers, and pesticides, reducing waste and increasing crop yields. With the help of drones, smart sensors, and machine learning algorithms, farmers can make more informed decisions, monitor crops in real-time, and predict optimal conditions for plant growth.

Drones for Crop Monitoring

Drones have become indispensable tools for precision agriculture. Equipped with high-resolution cameras and multispectral sensors, drones can fly over fields and collect detailed data on crop conditions. This data, analyzed through AI algorithms, provides crucial insights into the health of plants, detecting problems such as diseases, pests, or water stress in real-time.

Practical Example:

A drone flies over a wheat field, capturing multispectral images. By analyzing these images, an AI algorithm can detect areas where plants show signs of stress, such as yellowing leaves, indicating a possible nutrient deficiency or the presence of pests. With this information, the farmer can intervene promptly, applying fertilizers or pesticides only where needed, reducing excessive chemical use and costs.

Smart Sensors for Resource Optimization

In addition to drones, precision agriculture uses smart sensors installed in the soil or on farming machinery to monitor parameters like soil moisture, temperature, and air quality. These sensors provide real-time data that can be used to optimize irrigation and fertilizer usage.

Practical Example:

In a cornfield, soil sensors constantly monitor moisture levels. When these levels drop below a critical threshold, an AI-powered smart irrigation system automatically activates, delivering the exact amount of water needed. This system not only prevents water waste but also avoids over-irrigation, which can harm the plants.

Benefits of Precision Agriculture

- Resource Optimization: Targeted use of water, fertilizers, and pesticides reduces costs and environmental impact.

- Continuous Monitoring: AI-based technologies allow farmers to monitor crops in real-time and intervene quickly.

- Increased Yield: With more informed decisions, farmers can maximize crop yields and improve quality.

Precision agriculture is changing the farming sector, making agricultural practices more efficient and sustainable. Thanks to AI, drones, and smart sensors, farmers can optimize resources and improve crop performance, contributing to smarter and more responsible food production.

TRANSPORTATION AND AUTONOMOUS DRIVING

Artificial intelligence (AI) is deeply transforming the transportation sector, particularly with autonomous driving and intelligent traffic management systems. Self-driving cars, powered by deep learning algorithms, advanced sensors, and powerful onboard computers, are paving the way for a future where vehicles can move safely and efficiently without human intervention. Companies like Tesla are at the forefront of developing these revolutionary technologies.

How Autonomous Driving Works

Autonomous cars use a combination of sensors (such as cameras, radar, and lidar), machine learning algorithms, and neural networks to "see" and "understand" their surroundings. These systems can detect objects, road signs, vehicles, pedestrians, and any other elements present on the road. AI continuously processes this information in real-time, making decisions such as accelerating, braking, steering, and even choosing alternate routes based on traffic conditions.

At the heart of autonomous driving are deep learning algorithms, which learn from vast amounts of data collected from real-world vehicles on the road. During training, the algorithms learn to recognize common patterns and situations, such as when a car is about to change lanes, or more complex behaviors like pedestrians at intersections. Every time an autonomous car drives, it collects data that can be used to further improve the system, making it safer and smarter.

Example: Tesla and FSD (Full Self-Driving)

Tesla is one of the undisputed leaders in autonomous driving, thanks to its Full Self-Driving (FSD) system, a suite of features that allows the car to drive autonomously in almost any condition. Tesla uses a system based on cameras and neural networks to analyze the road in real-time, combining this information with GPS and high-resolution maps to navigate safely.

The FSD system is continuously improved through over-the-air software updates, allowing cars to learn new features and improve performance even after purchase. Tesla has adopted a vision-based approach, relying heavily on cameras to perceive the environment, as opposed to solutions that primarily use lidar.

To fully appreciate the power and capabilities of this system, I highly recommend watching some videos of the latest FSD versions in action on YouTube. It's impressive to see how the car handles complex situations, such as busy intersections, roundabouts, parking, or lane changes on highways, without any human intervention.

Intelligent Traffic Management Systems

Beyond autonomous driving, AI is also transforming how cities manage traffic. Intelligent traffic management systems use machine learning algorithms to analyze traffic flows in real-time, optimizing traffic light management, predicting congestion, and suggesting alternative routes to improve vehicle flow.

For example, in many major cities, traffic lights are connected to smart networks that adjust wait times based on the number of vehicles present. AI can gather data from cameras and road sensors and, in real-time, adjust traffic light timings to reduce congestion during peak hours. This not only reduces travel times but also helps lower CO_2 emissions through smoother traffic flow.

Benefits of Autonomous Driving and Intelligent Traffic Systems

1. Reduction in Traffic Accidents: Autonomous driving algorithms are designed to be highly responsive and are not subject to human distractions or errors, reducing the risk of accidents.

2. Improved Traffic Efficiency: With AI managing traffic and autonomous vehicles coordinating with each other, traffic becomes smoother, reducing congestion and wait times.

3. Time Savings: With autonomous driving, passengers can focus on other activities during the trip, making time spent in the car more productive.

4. Reduced Emissions: More efficient traffic means fewer idle vehicles and reduced fuel consumption, contributing to lower pollution.

Artificial intelligence is reshaping the future of transportation, bringing innovations such as autonomous cars and intelligent traffic management systems. Companies like Tesla are leading the way in developing these technologies, making autonomous driving an increasingly close reality. To fully appreciate how advanced these systems are, it's worth watching some of the videos available online showcasing the latest versions of Tesla's FSD: it's truly impressive to see what AI can do in the field of driving.

ARTIFICIAL INTELLIGENCE IN THE MILITARY FIELD

Artificial intelligence (AI) is rapidly transforming the military sector, introducing new technologies that are redefining how wars are fought and defense operations are conducted. From strategic planning to surveillance, from autonomous drones to cybersecurity systems, AI is revolutionizing every aspect of military operations while raising ethical and legal concerns.

Applications of AI in the Military

1. Drones and Autonomous Systems

   One of the most significant developments in the use of AI in the military is the deployment of drones and autonomous vehicles. AI-powered drones can operate without the need for direct human control, conducting reconnaissance, surveillance, and even targeting specific objectives. These drones can analyze their environment, identify potential threats, and react quickly, enhancing the effectiveness of field operations.

An example is the use of UAVs (Unmanned Aerial Vehicles), already employed in numerous military missions. AI enables these aircraft to make autonomous decisions, such as changing flight paths based on battlefield conditions or selecting targets to strike. The use of autonomous drones offers significant tactical advantages, reducing the need to expose soldiers to dangerous situations.

2. Surveillance and Reconnaissance

   AI is also crucial in surveillance and reconnaissance systems. AI algorithms can quickly analyze vast amounts of data from satellites, cameras, and sensors, identifying suspicious movements or hostile military activity. These surveillance systems can continuously and accurately monitor large geographical areas, making military forces more efficient in gathering and analyzing intelligence.

AI technology can also enhance facial recognition systems and enemy movement tracking, offering a strategic advantage to armed forces. Real-time data analysis systems allow the military to respond more rapidly to threats and predict adversary moves with greater accuracy.

3. Simulations and Strategic Planning

   AI is used in war simulations to predict potential outcomes of military operations. AI-based simulations can model various battle scenarios, considering thousands of variables, allowing commanders to make more informed decisions. These simulations not only improve strategic planning but also enable soldiers to train in highly realistic simulated environments.

AI can analyze data collected during these simulations and provide suggestions to optimize strategies, making resource management more efficient and improving coordination between different military units.

4. Cyberdefense

   Another area where AI is proving effective is cyberdefense. AI systems can detect cyberattacks in real-time by analyzing network traffic patterns and identifying suspicious activities. Machine learning algorithms allow defense systems to anticipate cyber threats and respond automatically, protecting critical infrastructures, military communication systems, and sensitive data.

Protecting military networks from cyberattacks is crucial, as modern warfare is fought not only on traditional battlefields but also in cyberspace. In this context, AI represents one of the most powerful weapons in cyber warfare.

5. Military Robotics

Beyond drones, AI is driving significant advancements in military robotics. Autonomous robots can be used to perform logistical support missions, such as transporting heavy loads or conducting repairs in dangerous areas. Additionally, AI-equipped combat robots can be deployed in high-risk situations, such as demining operations or combat in confined spaces.

Ethical Issues and Challenges

While AI offers significant advantages in the military sector, it also raises ethical and legal concerns. The use of autonomous weapons, such as armed drones, raises crucial questions about who should be responsible for life-or-death decisions made by machines. Experts fear that AI could reduce human involvement in critical military decisions, increasing the risk of errors or uncontrolled escalation.

Moreover, the use of AI for mass surveillance could compromise privacy and human rights, especially in civilian contexts, where these technologies could be used to suppress dissent or limit personal freedoms.

HOW ARTIFICIAL INTELLIGENCE CAN HELP PEOPLE WITH DISABILITIES

Artificial intelligence (AI) offers enormous potential to improve the lives of people with disabilities, helping them overcome physical, sensory, and cognitive barriers that may limit their autonomy. Through AI-based tools and technologies, solutions can be created to enable people with disabilities to live more independently, facilitating their integration into society and the workforce. Let's explore how AI can make a difference in various areas.

1. Mobility and Physical Access

For people with mobility impairments, AI is revolutionizing how they move and interact with the world around them. Some of the most important innovations include:

- Smart mobility systems, such as autonomous wheelchairs. These wheelchairs, equipped with AI and sensors, can navigate autonomously through complex environments, avoiding obstacles and helping the user reach their desired destination, reducing the need for external assistance.

- Robotic exoskeletons, devices that help people with paralysis or muscle weakness walk. AI analyzes body movements to provide targeted support, improving mobility.

2. Assisted Communication

People with speech or cognitive disabilities can greatly benefit from AI through tools that facilitate communication and interaction with others:

- Voice assistants like Siri, Alexa, and Google Assistant help those with motor or visual impairments interact with technological devices through voice commands, simplifying daily tasks such as sending messages, managing home activities, and obtaining information.

- Augmentative communication systems use AI to convert neural signals or eye movements into words, allowing people with severe disabilities, such as those with ALS (Amyotrophic Lateral Sclerosis), to communicate effectively.

3. Visual Accessibility

For people with visual impairments, AI is creating new ways to perceive the surrounding environment:

- Visual recognition apps, such as Microsoft's Seeing AI, use a smartphone's camera to describe the environment, read text, or identify faces, objects, and places. This helps blind individuals navigate independently and perform daily tasks.

- AI-equipped smart glasses, like those developed by OrCam, can describe what is happening around the user, reading text and recognizing faces or products.

4. Hearing Accessibility

For people who are deaf or hard of hearing, AI is transforming how they perceive sounds through:

- Automatic captions for videos and real-time conversations, provided by platforms like Google Meet or Microsoft Teams, which use speech recognition algorithms to transcribe conversations.

- Sign language translation apps that use AI to convert sign language into text or voice, facilitating communication between deaf and hearing individuals.

5. Cognitive Support

People with cognitive disabilities, such as those with autism or learning disorders, can benefit from AI through:

- Learning assistance apps, which use algorithms to personalize educational content based on individual needs and abilities, making learning more accessible and less stressful.

- Intelligent virtual assistants for daily task management, which help people with cognitive difficulties organize their day by reminding them of appointments, tasks, and medications.

6. Inclusion in the Workplace

Artificial intelligence can also be a tool for promoting the inclusion of people with disabilities in the workforce. Technologies such as:

- Voice recognition software and automation tools allow people with motor or visual disabilities to use computers and technological devices to work with greater autonomy.

- Predictive analysis tools can be used to personalize career paths and suggest job roles compatible with the skills and limitations of people with disabilities.

7. Home Assistance and Daily Life

Finally, AI can significantly improve the home life of people with disabilities:

- AI-powered smart home systems, such as smart thermostats, lights, and locks, can be controlled via voice commands or apps, offering a higher level of independence.

- Domestic assistant robots, designed to help with daily tasks, can assist with household chores such as meal preparation, cleaning, and health monitoring.

CHAPTER 6: AI in Everyday Life

Many of us think of artificial intelligence (AI) as a futuristic technology, still far from our daily lives. In reality, AI is already deeply integrated into our everyday activities, often without us realizing it. For years, we've been using AI-powered tools and services to simplify our lives: from voice assistants like Alexa and Google Assistant to recommendations on Netflix or Amazon, and even the navigation systems we use to find the best route. In this chapter, we will explore concrete examples of how AI is already a part of our daily routine, showing that the future is much closer than we think.

VIRTUAL ASSISTANTS (SIRI, ALEXA, GOOGLE ASSISTANT)

Virtual assistants like Siri, Alexa, and Google Assistant are among the most visible manifestations of artificial intelligence in everyday life. These tools allow us to interact with technology naturally, simply by using our voice. But how do they understand our requests and respond correctly? All of this is possible thanks to advanced natural language processing (NLP) techniques, which enable AI systems to interpret, analyze, and generate responses in human language.

How Do Voice Assistants Work?

1. Speech Recognition: When you speak to a voice assistant, the first step is to convert your voice into text. This operation is called speech-to-text. Virtual assistants use AI algorithms to recognize the words you are

saying, even in the presence of different accents or background noise. These systems are trained on millions of voice samples to improve their ability to correctly interpret various pronunciations.

2. Natural Language Processing (NLP): Once your voice is converted into text, the core system kicks in: natural language processing. Voice assistants use deep learning models to understand the meaning of what you've said. This process is not simple, as human sentences can be ambiguous or contain words with different meanings depending on the context. For example, if you say, "Turn on the light in the living room," the assistant must:

   o Recognize the requested action ("turn on").

   o Identify the object to act on ("light").

   o Understand the spatial context ("in the living room"). Thanks to NLP, the assistant can "understand" the intent behind the words and convert them into specific actions.

3. Response or Action: Once the request is understood, the virtual assistant takes action. If you've asked for information, like "What's the weather tomorrow?", the assistant uses cloud computing to access weather data and return a coherent response. If you made a practical request, such as "Turn off the TV," the assistant sends a command to the smart home devices to carry out the action.

Examples of How They Work

- Apple's Siri can manage complex operations like sending messages, setting alarms, or searching for information on the internet. For example, if you say, "Send a message to Mario: I'm on my way," Siri correctly interprets who the recipient is and the content of the message.

- Amazon's Alexa, in addition to answering questions and controlling home devices, can manage personalized routines, executing a series of preset commands like turning on the lights, starting music, and adjusting the thermostat in the morning.

- Google Assistant is particularly known for its ability to provide detailed answers integrated with Google's search engine. If you ask, "How far is the nearest restaurant?" Assistant will not only tell you the distance but can also show you the map and calculate the arrival time based on traffic.

Continuous Learning and Improvement

Voice assistants are not static. Every time we interact with them, the AI collects feedback data to improve its responses over time. These systems use machine learning techniques to refine their abilities and improve performance, becoming increasingly precise in recognizing voices, understanding requests, and anticipating users' needs.

Limitations and Challenges

Despite the progress, voice assistants still face some challenges. One of the main ones is context: understanding longer, more complex conversations or ambiguous questions can be difficult. For example, if you ask sequential questions like, "Who won the last Juventus match?" and then immediately ask, "And when will they play again?", the assistant must understand that "they" refers to Juventus. Some assistants are good at maintaining context, while others may make mistakes.

Virtual assistants like Siri, Alexa, and Google Assistant have become indispensable companions in daily life, simplifying our interactions with technology through natural language processing. Even if we don't always notice their role, these AIs are making our lives more convenient and connected, continually improving their ability to understand and respond to our requests.

RECOMMENDATION ALGORITHMS (NETFLIX, AMAZON, SPOTIFY...)

Recommendation algorithms are one of the most widespread applications of artificial intelligence in everyday life. Platforms like Netflix, Amazon, and many other online services use AI to analyze user preferences and behaviors, providing personalized suggestions for movies, TV series, or products. These algorithms not only enhance the user experience but also help companies keep their audience engaged and increase sales.

How Do Recommendation Algorithms Work?

Recommendation algorithms rely on advanced machine learning techniques that allow them to identify patterns in data. Their functioning is based on three main approaches:

1. Collaborative Filtering: This approach is based on interactions between users and content. If a user has enjoyed certain movies or products, the system looks for other users with similar tastes and recommends content they might also like. For example, if a user has watched and liked several romantic comedies, Netflix might suggest other romantic comedies that were appreciated by users with similar tastes.

2. Content-Based Filtering: In this case, the algorithm analyzes the characteristics of the content itself (such as the genre of a movie, the main actors, or the plot) and compares it with what the user has already enjoyed. If a user has watched many action movies, the algorithm will try to suggest films of the same genre with similar characteristics.

3. Hybrid Models: Many platforms, like Netflix and Amazon, use a hybrid approach, combining collaborative filtering with content-based filtering to provide more accurate recommendations. These models take into account both the user's personal preferences and what similar users enjoy.

Practical Examples: Netflix and Amazon

- Netflix uses sophisticated recommendation algorithms to suggest movies and TV series that might interest the user. Every time you watch a movie, leave a review, or stop watching something halfway, Netflix collects this data to build a preference profile. Through this analysis, the platform can suggest new content that matches your tastes and continuously improve its recommendations as your profile evolves.

- Amazon uses similar algorithms to suggest products based on your previous purchases, items viewed, and reviews. Amazon's algorithm also considers the behavior of other shoppers: if many users who bought a particular product also purchased another, Amazon might suggest the same item to you, increasing the chances of a sale.

Impact on Users and Benefits

Recommendation algorithms offer a personalized experience, simplifying the discovery of new content and products that might otherwise go unnoticed. For companies, these systems increase user engagement, encouraging them to spend more time on the platform or purchase more products. For example, Netflix can keep users engaged by suggesting new shows based on their tastes, while Amazon boosts sales by recommending relevant products.

AI-based recommendation algorithms have become a key component of online platforms, enhancing the user experience and optimizing content and product offerings. Thanks to advanced machine learning techniques, services like Netflix and Amazon can provide increasingly accurate and personalized suggestions, keeping users engaged and satisfied.

SOCIAL MEDIA AND PERSONALIZATION

Artificial intelligence (AI) plays a central role in personalizing social media feeds on platforms like Facebook, Instagram, X, TikTok, and many others. Every time you scroll through your feed, AI works behind the scenes to decide which posts, videos, or ads to show you, based on factors such as your past interactions and the content you've viewed or engaged with most frequently. This personalization process has transformed social media into a digital space perfectly tailored to your interests and behaviors.

How AI Personalizes the Feed

Social platforms use machine learning algorithms to analyze user behavior and create personalized experiences. These algorithms primarily rely on three key aspects:

1. Past Interactions: Every like, comment, share, or click is recorded by the algorithm. This helps build a detailed profile of your interests and preferences. If you often engage with posts from a particular friend or specific pages, the algorithm will tend to show you similar posts more frequently.

2. Viewing Time: How long you spend viewing certain content is another fundamental factor. If you scroll quickly past a post, AI interprets that you're not interested. Conversely, if you watch a video in full or spend more time on an image, the algorithm understands that this type of content interests you and will try to show you similar posts in the future.

3. Similar Behaviors: Social media algorithms also analyze the interactions of users with behaviors similar to yours. If many people with your interests start following a new page or engaging with new content, AI is likely to suggest the same to you.

Practical Examples: Facebook and Instagram

- Facebook uses a complex algorithm to select the content you see in your feed, showing posts it deems most relevant. This can include status updates from friends you interact with most, posts from pages you follow, or ads based on your previous searches.

- Instagram uses similar algorithms for its main feed and the Explore section. Here, every interaction, view, and time spent on certain content influences what you will see in the future. The goal is to keep you engaged by showing content that captures your attention.

The Influence of Social Media and Risks

While personalized social media makes browsing more enjoyable and engaging, it also carries significant risks regarding how these platforms can influence users. Algorithms, designed to keep you engaged as long as possible, often show content that reinforces your opinions or triggers strong emotions like anger or surprise. This phenomenon can create an "information bubble," where users are only exposed to content that confirms their beliefs, ignoring alternative perspectives.

Additionally, heavy reliance on algorithms to decide what you see can lead to manipulation of information. Platforms can influence how we perceive reality by promoting certain content over others based on commercial or political motives.

For example, Facebook has been at the center of debates on how its algorithms influenced political elections and contributed to the spread of fake news. Instagram, on the other hand, has been accused of contributing to self-esteem issues among young people by constantly showing images that promote unrealistic standards of life or beauty, chosen to generate more interactions.

These aspects raise serious ethical questions about how much power social media has in shaping our thoughts, tastes, and even our political or consumer decisions. Platforms are not just spaces for sharing but also manipulation machines powered by AI, exploiting our preferences to hold our attention for as long as possible. While this is a complex issue deserving a book of its own, we will explore it further in this text.

AI algorithms that personalize social media are powerful tools that make our experience more engaging and customized. However, their potential to influence our opinions and habits should not be underestimated. While browsing through content that interests us is useful and fun, it's important to remain aware of the power these algorithms have in shaping what we see and, ultimately, how we think.

SMART HOME AND HOME AUTOMATION

Smart home and home automation technology is transforming our homes into increasingly intelligent and connected spaces, thanks to the use of artificial intelligence (AI). These automated systems make daily home management more convenient and secure, allowing control of everything from temperature to security systems simply through an app, voice commands, or fully automatic settings.

How Home Automation Works

Home automation relies on the integration of connected devices that communicate with each other through a central network, often controlled by voice assistants like Alexa, Google Assistant, or Siri. AI plays a crucial role in optimizing these systems, learning from users' preferences and improving the overall efficiency of the home.

1. Temperature Control: One of the most common uses of AI in smart homes is intelligent temperature control. Devices like the Nest thermostat use machine learning algorithms to learn users' daily habits, automatically adjusting the temperature based on schedules and preferences. For example, the system may lower the heating when it detects the house is empty and raise it just before the owners return, improving comfort and reducing energy costs.

2. Lighting Management: AI can also optimize smart lighting. Systems like Philips Hue allow lights to be automated based on the time of day, external brightness, or personal habits. The lighting can be adjusted automatically based on whether people are in the rooms or set to follow specific routines, such as turning off all lights at night or turning them on at sunrise.

3. Security Systems: Security is another area where AI makes a difference. Smart surveillance systems, such as Ring security cameras or smart doorbells, use AI to distinguish between suspicious activity and normal movements. The cameras can send real-time notifications if they detect unusual people or sounds and even recognize familiar faces, reducing false alarms.

4. Voice Assistants: Voice assistants like Alexa, Google Assistant, and Siri serve as central hubs for managing all smart devices. With a simple voice command, it's possible to turn on lights, control appliances, or adjust the temperature. These assistants, thanks to AI, learn from user interactions and become increasingly capable of understanding complex or customized commands.

Practical Example: Home Automation

Imagine coming home after a long day of work: thanks to AI-powered home automation, your house could already be prepared for your arrival. The thermostat has heated the environment to the perfect temperature, the lights turn on as you enter, and the voice assistant gives you an update on the news or weather. If you have a security camera, you can also check via smartphone who passed by your house during the day.

Benefits of Smart Homes

- Energy Efficiency: Smart systems automatically regulate heating, lighting, and electronic devices, reducing energy waste.

- Comfort and Convenience: With a few voice commands or pre-configured settings, many household tasks can be automated.

- Improved Security: Smart surveillance systems protect the home and provide constant monitoring, even when you're not there.

AI-powered smart homes and home automation are making our living spaces more intelligent, secure, and efficient. With devices that learn from our habits and automatically manage the main aspects of daily life, smart homes offer a personalized and increasingly automated living experience, making our lives simpler and more comfortable.

GAMING AND ARTIFICIAL INTELLIGENCE

Artificial intelligence (AI) has had a significant impact on the gaming world, making video games more immersive and dynamic. From non-player characters (NPCs) to games that adapt to player behavior, AI has become a crucial component in creating increasingly realistic, interactive, and challenging gaming experiences.

Intelligent NPCs

One of the most common uses of AI in video games is managing non-player characters (NPCs). NPCs are computer-controlled characters that interact with the player or the game environment. In the past, NPCs followed predefined and repetitive patterns, making their actions predictable. With the introduction of AI, NPCs have become smarter, reacting dynamically to player actions and adapting their behavior in real-time.

For example, in strategy games like Age of Empires or StarCraft, AI can plan complex strategies based on the player's moves, creating a more engaging challenge. In role-playing games (RPGs) like The Elder Scrolls or Fallout, NPCs not only interact with the player based on their choices but can also perform autonomous actions, such as working, fighting, or socializing with other NPCs.

AI that Adapts to Player Behavior

Another innovative aspect of AI in gaming is its ability to adapt to player behavior. In games like Left 4 Dead or Alien: Isolation, AI observes how the player behaves and modifies the difficulty or dynamics of the game accordingly. If a player is particularly skilled, AI can increase the challenge by generating more aggressive enemies or creating more complex situations. Conversely, if the player is struggling, AI may reduce the difficulty or offer invisible assistance to keep the experience enjoyable without frustration.

This adaptability makes games more engaging, as they offer a continuous, personalized challenge. AI can anticipate player actions and respond in ways that keep the game interesting, preventing it from becoming monotonous or too difficult.

AI-Based Games

Beyond NPCs and dynamic adaptations, some games use AI as the core component of the gameplay. For example, in Hello Neighbor, AI learns the player's habits and modifies traps and paths to surprise the player at each attempt. This approach makes every game session unique and unpredictable, offering a highly personalized gaming experience.

Moreover, AI is used to create procedural worlds in games. In titles like Minecraft or No Man's Sky, AI automatically generates vast, unique worlds for each player, ensuring that no two games are alike.

Benefits of AI in Gaming

The use of AI in video games has brought about significant advantages:

- More realistic gaming experiences: Intelligent NPCs and AI-based game dynamics make the game environment more lively and believable.

- Increased replayability: AI that adapts to the player provides new challenges, extending the game's longevity.

- Personalized gameplay: AI-based games offer unique experiences tailored to each player, enhancing interaction and immersion.

From intelligent NPCs to games that adapt to player behavior, AI has enhanced gaming experiences, making them more dynamic and personalized. As technology advances, we can expect even more sophisticated games, with AI continuing to play a fundamental role.

CHAPTER 7: Ethical and Social Challenges of AI

In this chapter, I want to explore some of the most relevant ethical challenges related to artificial intelligence, though without aiming to provide definitive answers. Ethics is subjective, and it's impossible to find a universal answer that suits everyone. What I want to do here is present some real questions and dilemmas, leaving it to you to reflect and form your own opinion without external influence.

In fact, who's to say I'm not an AI designed to make you think in a certain way? Jokes aside, this chapter offers an opportunity to explore the ethical implications of AI, from privacy issues to labor and information control.

PRIVACY AND DATA SECURITY

Artificial intelligence (AI) has brought enormous benefits to many sectors, but one of the most important challenges involves privacy and data security. For AI to function effectively, it requires vast amounts of data, much of which can include personal and sensitive information. This reliance on data raises concerns about how it is collected, stored, and used, especially in contexts where control and surveillance can become too invasive.

Personal Data Management

AI algorithms are built to analyze and learn from large datasets, often consisting of personal information such as online activity, consumer preferences, spending habits, and even biometric data like fingerprints and facial recognition. These data are used to improve services, personalize user experiences, and make more accurate predictions. However, this creates a significant problem: how much privacy are we willing to sacrifice for greater convenience?

Example:

When a fitness app collects data on our movements and physical conditions, we generally agree because it provides a useful service. But what happens to that data once it's collected? Can it be shared with third parties without our explicit consent? This is one of the major weak points in data management by AI systems.

ENVIRONMENTAL IMPACT

The environmental issue related to artificial intelligence (AI) has become an increasingly important topic, as the development and use of AI require a significant amount of energy resources. Training and executing large-scale AI models, particularly those based on deep neural networks (deep learning), have a substantial environmental impact, mainly due to the high energy consumption needed to run such calculations.

1. High Energy Consumption

Training AI models requires enormous computing power, often supported by GPUs, TPUs, and large servers. Each training phase can last days or weeks, with continuous energy use.

- Large models like those behind ChatGPT or language models like GPT-3 require millions of parameters to be trained and updated. Some estimates suggest that training a large deep learning model can consume the same amount of energy that an average American household uses in a year.

2. Carbon Emissions

In addition to energy consumption, many of the resources needed to power data centers and servers hosting AI models come from non-renewable sources, such as coal and natural gas. This contributes to CO_2 emissions, exacerbating the climate crisis.

- For example, a 2019 study estimated that training a single large deep learning model produced over 284 tons of CO_2, equivalent to the emissions produced by about five cars throughout their entire life.

3. Data Centers and Cooling

Data centers, which house the servers used to train and run AI models, require significant amounts of energy not only for computation but also for cooling. Overheating is a serious issue, and many data centers use advanced cooling systems, which further increase energy consumption.

- Some large cloud providers, like Google and Microsoft, are working to reduce this impact by using renewable energy sources to power their data centers, but the demand for energy continues to grow.

4. Impact of Devices

Beyond servers and data centers, AI is integrated into a wide range of smart devices (smartphones, voice assistants, autonomous cars), which contribute to environmental impact during their production and use.

- For example, the widespread adoption of voice assistants like Amazon Alexa or Google Assistant involves constant use of cloud resources to process voice commands and provide responses, increasing the load on data centers.

5. More Efficient Models

Fortunately, the scientific community and tech companies are working to reduce the environmental impact of AI. Some approaches include:

- Algorithm efficiency: Researchers are developing more energy-efficient machine learning and deep learning algorithms, requiring less computing power to achieve similar results.

- Smaller models: Instead of using enormous deep learning models, the use of smaller, more efficient models optimized for specific tasks can reduce energy consumption.

- Quantization and pruning: Techniques that reduce the complexity of AI models without compromising performance, decreasing computational load and energy consumption.

6. Shift to Renewable Energy

Many major AI and cloud service providers, such as Amazon Web Services, Google Cloud, and Microsoft Azure, are investing in renewable energy sources to power their data centers. The goal is to reduce the carbon footprint and make AI more environmentally sustainable.

- Google, for example, has committed to achieving 100% renewable energy for all of its data centers. This is an important step toward reducing environmental impact, although overall energy consumption continues to rise.

7. Recycling and Disposal of Devices

Another important aspect of AI's environmental impact concerns the production and disposal of electronic devices. Many AI-based devices, such as smartphones, smart speakers, and other IoT devices, have a relatively short lifespan and generate electronic waste (e-waste).

- A solution to reduce this impact is to promote the recycling of electronic devices and improve manufacturing processes to make these devices more durable and easier to repair.

AI offers extraordinary opportunities, but it also has a significant environmental cost. The growing energy use to train and run large AI models and the role of data centers represent challenges that must be addressed to ensure AI is sustainable in the long term. Fortunately, the industry is making progress in making AI more energy-efficient and adopting renewable energy solutions. However, these efforts must continue to grow to balance technological innovation with environmental responsibility.

Surveillance Risks

One of the most concerning risks is the increasing use of AI technologies for surveillance, particularly facial recognition. This technology allows identification by analyzing a person's face and comparing it to a database of images. In many countries, facial recognition is already used in public spaces like airports, stations, and squares with the aim of ensuring security and preventing crime.

However, there's a darker side to it. Mass surveillance through facial recognition can violate individuals' right to privacy. In China, for example, facial recognition is used to monitor citizens' movements and enforce a social credit system, where "non-compliant" behavior can result in negative consequences, such as being denied access to public services or loans. This raises serious concerns about government control and personal freedom.

Example: In many Western countries, facial recognition has been tested at sporting events or demonstrations to identify suspects or prevent crimes. But the lack of proper regulations means that this technology can be used for other purposes, such as monitoring innocent individuals, thereby endangering their privacy.

Data Security

Another critical aspect is data security. AI-based technologies collect vast amounts of data, making them an attractive target for cybercriminals. Cyberattacks aimed at stealing personal, financial, or health data are on the rise, and companies managing this data don't always implement adequate security measures.

Example: If a bank uses AI to analyze spending behaviors and optimize financial services, customer data must be carefully protected. However, if this data is breached due to a security flaw, the damage to the customer can be enormous, causing not only financial loss but also harm to their reputation and trust in the company.

Regulation and Awareness

Globally, many governments are working to develop regulations to protect citizens' privacy in the AI era. The General Data Protection Regulation (GDPR) of the European Union is one of the most well-known examples, setting strict limits on how companies can collect and use personal data.

Despite this, technology advances much faster than laws, leaving many gray areas. For example, in the United States, regulations vary significantly from state to state, making it difficult for citizens to know how their data is being handled.

Privacy and data security in the age of artificial intelligence are fundamental issues that require constant attention. AI offers enormous benefits, but the risks associated with personal data management and surveillance are equally significant. It is important to strike a balance between technological progress and the protection of individual rights by properly regulating data usage and raising awareness among citizens about the potential risks of AI.

BIAS AND DISCRIMINATION

One of the biggest risks associated with artificial intelligence is the possibility that algorithms could perpetuate or even amplify existing societal biases. Although AI is often perceived as neutral, many machine learning systems are trained on historical data that reflects racial, gender, or class biases. These biases can significantly influence decisions made by algorithms, leading to discrimination in various sectors.

Gender Bias in Recruitment Systems

A significant example occurred with an AI-based recruitment system developed by HireVue, a video interview platform that uses artificial intelligence to analyze candidates' facial expressions, tone of voice, and body language. The algorithm was designed to evaluate and rank candidates based on these signals, but issues of bias emerged.

HireVue's algorithms were criticized for the risk of perpetuating gender and racial biases, as the models were trained on data reflecting existing stereotypes. For instance, candidates who do not conform to certain cultural standards of body language or tone of voice may be penalized, regardless of their actual competence. This can lead to discrimination against individuals from minority or different cultural backgrounds, who may have a different communication style compared to the dominant majority. The company responded to the criticism by claiming it had taken measures to reduce biases, but concerns about the fairness of the system remained.

Racial Bias in Facial Recognition

Another emblematic example of bias is found in facial recognition systems. Studies conducted by MIT and Stanford University have shown that many facial recognition technologies have significantly higher error rates when identifying people of color compared to lighter-skinned individuals. In particular, Black women are the most penalized group, with much higher error rates than white men.

This problem arises from the fact that facial recognition algorithms are trained on biased datasets, primarily consisting of images of white people. When applied in real-world contexts, these systems risk amplifying racial inequalities, especially when used in security or public surveillance applications.

In the United States, there have been instances where Black individuals were wrongfully arrested due to errors in facial recognition. These cases highlight how racial discrimination can be unconsciously perpetuated and amplified by supposedly neutral algorithms.

Bias in Financial Systems

AI can also introduce bias in the financial sector. For example, credit scoring models used by banks to assess clients' creditworthiness can be influenced by historical data that reflects socioeconomic or racial biases. If a person comes from a historically disadvantaged neighborhood, they might receive a lower credit score due to unjustified correlations in the data, even if they have a stable income or a consistent repayment history.

A practical example emerged with the Apple Card credit scoring system, developed by Apple in collaboration with Goldman Sachs. Several users reported that, under the same conditions, women were receiving significantly lower credit limits than men. This issue was brought to light by public figures, including Apple co-founder Steve Wozniak, who noted that his wife had received a much lower credit limit than he did, despite having similar financial conditions.

In this case, gender bias was embedded in the credit evaluation algorithm, leading to unfair treatment for many applicants. Although Apple and Goldman Sachs claimed not to engage in gender discrimination, the issue highlighted how biases in historical data can be transferred to algorithms, resulting in real-world discrimination.

The Root of the Problem

The fundamental problem is that AI algorithms learn from historical data. If the data contains biases, the algorithm will simply reproduce them. These systems cannot distinguish between legitimate correlations and hidden biases, which can lead to discriminatory decisions in critical areas like employment, finance, and public security.

The lack of transparency in algorithms, often described as "black boxes," further complicates the issue, making it difficult to identify and correct the biases present in AI models.

ALGORITHM TRANSPARENCY

One of the central topics in the debate surrounding artificial intelligence is algorithm transparency, which refers to the ability to understand how an algorithm arrives at a specific decision. This issue becomes particularly relevant with the use of complex algorithms such as deep learning models, often described, as mentioned earlier, as "black boxes," because even experts find it difficult to comprehend how decisions are made.

Deep learning algorithms, for example, use deep neural networks that simulate the workings of the human brain to recognize patterns and make predictions. However, the internal process leading to a specific decision is often opaque. In many cases, even the developers themselves cannot explain exactly why the algorithm made a particular choice, as neural networks operate by processing thousands or millions of parameters in a non-linear way.

The "Black Box" of Deep Learning

The term "black box" refers to the opaque nature of AI algorithms, particularly with advanced technologies such as deep learning. These algorithms autonomously learn from data, and the more complex the model becomes, the harder it is for humans to trace the decision-making path.

A practical example is found in healthcare, where AI algorithms are used to analyze medical data and make diagnoses. While deep learning models can be extremely effective in detecting diseases, such as in the early detection of breast cancer through medical imaging, the lack of transparency can be a significant barrier. If a doctor cannot explain how the algorithm determined that a patient has a disease, it becomes difficult for them to make decisions based on these recommendations. This can lead to a loss of trust in the system.

In some cases, the lack of transparency can have legal consequences. For example, in the United States, concerns have been raised about the use of predictive algorithms in the judicial system, where AI is used to assess the recidivism risk of criminals. Opaque algorithms suggesting decisions on parole or sentencing can raise concerns about justice and discrimination, especially if it's impossible to understand the basis for those decisions.

Why Transparency Matters

Algorithm transparency is crucial for several reasons. First, it increases trust from users and consumers. If people understand how AI works and the basis on which decisions are made, they will be more inclined to accept and rely on it. Transparency also helps identify any errors or biases in algorithms, allowing developers to correct problems before they cause real harm.

Additionally, transparency is essential for ethical accountability. If an algorithm makes a wrong or unjust decision, how can responsibility be determined if it's unclear how the decision was made? This is especially important in sectors like healthcare, finance, or the legal system, where AI-based decisions can have a significant impact on people's lives.

Toward Greater Transparency

To address this issue, AI experts are developing tools to improve algorithm explainability, often referred to as "explainable AI" (XAI). These approaches aim to clarify AI's internal decision-making processes without compromising the system's effectiveness. The goal is to create AI models that are not only powerful and accurate but also understandable and verifiable by humans.

Increasing transparency in AI algorithms is essential to ensure the ethical and responsible use of the technology, especially in sectors that require high reliability and social responsibility.

EMPLOYMENT AND AUTOMATION

Artificial intelligence (AI) and automation are significantly transforming the world of work, creating new opportunities but also raising major challenges. On the one hand, automation promises increased efficiency and productivity, but on the other, it raises concerns about job security, with many workers fearing that machines or algorithms will replace them. This dynamic has sparked a broad debate on the impact automation will have on various industries and the skills that will be needed in the future.

Sectors at Risk

One of the key aspects of automation is its ability to replace repetitive and predictable tasks, especially in industrial and manufacturing sectors. The growing adoption of industrial robots and AI-based technologies has already begun to profoundly change production methods.

- Manufacturing: The manufacturing industry is probably the most affected by automation. Processes that previously required human intervention, such as assembly, quality control, or logistics, are increasingly being managed by intelligent robots. For example, in automotive factories, robots can assemble vehicles with millimeter precision, reducing errors and costs. The result is a decreased demand for skilled workers in these areas, but an increased need for specialized technicians to maintain and manage the robots.

- Logistics and Warehousing: Automation has also had a massive impact on the logistics and warehousing sector. Companies like Amazon use robots to move goods within their warehouses, speeding up delivery times and reducing the cost of human labor. However, this has raised concerns about how automation might replace low-skilled jobs, such as warehouse workers and handlers.

- Financial Services: Automation is revolutionizing the financial services sector as well. Tasks traditionally performed by financial analysts or bank operators, such as loan processing or transaction management, are increasingly handled by AI algorithms capable of processing data faster and more accurately. This has reduced the demand for professionals engaged in repetitive tasks and has led to a reevaluation of the human role in financial institutions.

- Customer Service: The field of customer service is also heavily influenced by automation, with the introduction of chatbots and virtual assistants handling basic customer requests. These systems, based on natural language processing (NLP) algorithms, can resolve simple issues without human intervention. This reduces the need for human staff for first-level tasks but creates the need for more advanced skills to handle complex cases or develop and maintain these technologies.

Impact of Automation on Skilled Labor

Despite concerns about job losses due to automation, not all sectors and professional roles are equally at risk. Tasks requiring creativity, critical thinking, and complex human interaction are much more difficult to automate. Professions in healthcare, education, research, and the creative arts remain largely dominated by human intervention, though AI can still provide support in various activities.

- Healthcare: In the healthcare sector, automation is used to improve diagnostics and treatments, but human presence remains essential. AI algorithms can help doctors interpret medical images or predict patients' responses to specific treatments, but human skills in direct patient interaction and final decision-making are irreplaceable.

- Engineering and Technology: Automation itself is creating new job opportunities in the technology sector. The development, programming, and maintenance of automated systems require highly specialized skills. The growing adoption of AI in businesses is increasing the demand for software engineers, data scientists, and AI experts. Additionally, cybersecurity experts are increasingly needed to ensure the safety of automated systems.

New Opportunities Created by Automation

While some sectors are at risk of losing jobs due to automation, others are emerging where AI is creating new opportunities. One of the main effects of automation is the creation of professions requiring new skills that did not exist just a few years ago.

- Maintenance and Management of Automated Systems: With the increasing use of robots and algorithms in industries, the demand for skilled personnel to maintain and optimize these systems is also rising. Maintaining industrial robots or managing machine learning algorithms requires a level of specialization and training that creates new job opportunities for technicians and engineers.

- Training and Reskilling: Another area offering new opportunities is training and reskilling. As the labor market evolves due to automation, there is a growing need to train workers on new technologies and skills. Companies are increasingly investing in training programs to prepare their employees to work with automated systems and AI.

- Creativity and Innovation: Even in sectors seemingly distant from technology, such as art, music, or writing, automation is creating new opportunities. AI algorithms are used to generate art, music, and digital content. While AI cannot fully replace human creativity, it can provide useful tools to enhance the creative process.

The Importance of Reskilling

A key factor in addressing the challenges of automation is workforce reskilling. While some jobs are at risk of being eliminated, others are emerging, but they require very different skills. It is crucial for governments and companies to invest in training programs to prepare workers to manage new technologies. This can reduce the negative impact of automation on employment and ensure a smoother transition to a technology-based economy.

In conclusion, automation is reshaping the employment landscape, creating both risks and opportunities. Repetitive and manual jobs are the most exposed to the risk of disappearing, while new professional roles related to managing, maintaining, and developing automated technologies are emerging. However, it is essential to promote continuous training to ensure that workers can adapt and thrive in this new work environment.

GOVERNANCE AND REGULATION

With the rapid spread of artificial intelligence (AI) across various sectors of society, there has been an increasing need to define norms and rules to ensure the ethical, safe, and transparent use of these technologies. AI regulation has become a priority for many governments and international organizations, seeking to balance technological innovation with the protection of individual rights, safety, and social justice. Examples such as the General Data Protection Regulation (GDPR) in Europe and the United Nations guidelines represent concrete efforts to address these challenges.

GDPR: The European Model

The European Union was one of the first entities to implement robust regulation for the use of data, and indirectly, AI, through the General Data Protection Regulation (GDPR), which came into effect in 2018. While the GDPR primarily focuses on personal data protection, it has significant implications for AI development and use, given that many AI systems rely on large amounts of personal data.

A key element of the GDPR is the right to transparency, requiring citizens to be informed about how their data is being used and to have the ability to access, correct, or delete such information. This principle poses a challenge for AI developers, as many machine learning and deep learning algorithms operate as "black boxes," where the internal decision-making process is not easily understandable. The GDPR mandates that automated decisions, such as those made by AI algorithms, must be explainable and transparent, pushing companies to develop "explainable AI" systems to meet these requirements.

Another relevant aspect of the GDPR is the protection against automated profiling. Citizens have the right not to be subject to decisions based solely on automated processes, including those using AI, if such decisions have a significant impact on their lives, such as loan approvals or employment selection. This has led many companies to reconsider the use of AI in critical processes, ensuring human oversight at key decision points.

UN Guidelines

The United Nations has also recognized the growing impact of AI and has published guidelines for the responsible use of these technologies. The UN's goal is to ensure that AI is developed and used in ways that respect human rights and promote sustainable development.

One of the UN's central concerns is the impact of AI on labor and social rights. The guidelines emphasize the importance of preventing automation and AI from increasing social and economic inequalities. Member states are encouraged to invest in reskilling programs for workers affected by automation and to develop policies ensuring that AI is used for the collective good.

Additionally, the UN has raised concerns about the use of AI-based surveillance technologies, such as facial recognition, which could violate privacy and freedom of expression. The guidelines call for greater democratic control and oversight of such technologies, especially when used by governments and public authorities.

Proposals for AI Regulation

Beyond the GDPR and UN guidelines, various countries are introducing regulations to govern AI and mitigate the risks associated with its use. For example, the European Union is working on an Artificial Intelligence Act that would classify AI systems based on their risk and impose stricter rules for high-risk applications, such as those used in healthcare, transportation, and law enforcement.

The EU's proposals include requiring companies to conduct a risk assessment before deploying AI systems, aiming to ensure they are safe, fair, and transparent. Companies developing high-risk AI systems will also need to demonstrate that their models are free from bias and that they respect citizens' fundamental rights.

Meanwhile, in the United States, AI regulation is still in its early stages, but several committees are considering the implementation of rules similar to those in Europe. In 2021, the National Institute of Standards and Technology (NIST) published a document outlining guidelines for managing risks in AI use, urging companies to be more transparent and accountable when implementing artificial intelligence systems.

Challenges and Opportunities of Regulation

AI regulation presents significant challenges. One of the main obstacles is finding a balance between promoting innovation and ensuring the safe and fair use of technology. Overly strict rules could slow technological progress, while overly permissive regulation could lead to negative consequences, such as discrimination, privacy violations, or the misuse of technology.

Another challenge is international cooperation. AI is a global technology and requires international coordination to avoid regulatory conflicts between countries. However, the emergence of regulations such as the GDPR and the UN's proposals marks an important step toward more ethical and responsible AI governance, with the aim of protecting human rights and ensuring that technology is used for the common good.

As we have seen, the issues and concerns surrounding AI are numerous, delicate, and occur at different levels. From privacy and transparency issues to employment impacts and the need for effective regulation, AI raises complex challenges that require careful consideration. However, it is important to remember that we are talking about a new, powerful, and rapidly evolving technology. It is normal for some issues to remain unresolved, especially in a context where changes are happening at an unprecedented pace.

In such a fast-changing world, information and awareness become crucial. This is why books like this one are important, as they offer an opportunity for deeper understanding, helping us navigate the challenges and opportunities that AI will bring into our lives.

In line with the above, in the next chapter, we will also address an ethical/creative dilemma, a topic that seemed unimaginable just a few years ago: the role of AI in creativity. It's a dilemma that forces us to reconsider one of the certainties we have always had. Until now, creativity has been considered the quality that most distinguishes humans from machines—the unique ability to imagine, invent, and create something new, which seemed impossible to replicate artificially.

Yet, with the advances in artificial intelligence, we find ourselves facing a new paradigm. AI is increasingly entering the fields of music, painting, writing, and many other forms of artistic expression, generating works and ideas in ways that make us wonder whether creativity is indeed an exclusively human trait. It is a question we never thought we would have to face, but today it becomes inevitable: machines not only can imitate but also seem capable of creating.

That said, we should not be prejudiced. AI is not necessarily a threat or a negative force for human creativity. As is often the case with new technologies, the key lies in how we use them. In this chapter, we are not only analyzing the phenomenon to identify risks but also to understand the opportunities it can create. AI can expand our creative horizons, offering unprecedented tools and possibilities that enrich and enhance art and culture.

CHAPTER 8: AI and Creativity

AI IN MUSIC

One of the creative fields where artificial intelligence (AI) is showing surprising results is music. In the past, musical composition was considered one of the purest expressions of human art, driven by emotion, creativity, and interpretation. However, AI has begun to play an important role in this area, demonstrating the ability to compose music independently based on specific inputs provided by users. An excellent example of this capability is AIVA (Artificial Intelligence Virtual Artist), one of the most advanced AIs in the field of music.

How AIVA Works

AIVA is an AI specialized in musical composition. Developed by the startup AIVA Technologies, this AI has been trained on a vast corpus of classical and modern works, understanding the musical structures of composers like Beethoven, Mozart, and Bach. Using deep learning algorithms, AIVA can analyze thousands of scores and identify musical patterns, harmonies, and chord progressions, which it then uses to create new compositions.

AIVA operates by interacting with specific inputs provided by users. For example, a composer or music producer can indicate a particular musical genre, style, or emotion to evoke, and AIVA will process these parameters to generate a musical piece that reflects these directions. AIVA's flexibility allows it to work in various musical genres, from classical to electronic music, jazz, and even film soundtracks.

Creating Soundtracks

One of the most promising fields for AI like AIVA is the creation of soundtracks for movies, video games, and advertisements. Soundtrack composition requires crafting atmospheres that accompany visuals or narratives, maintaining an emotional rhythm aligned with the action. AIVA can produce these compositions quickly and with a high degree of customization. By specifying the tone of the project (epic, romantic, dramatic, etc.), the length of the piece, and other specific parameters, the AI is capable of producing a suitable soundtrack.

In some cases, AIVA is used as a support tool for human composers. For example, a composer might use the AI to generate musical ideas or drafts, which can then be modified and refined by human hands. This accelerates the creative process, offering new sources of inspiration.

A New Tool for Composers

Although AIVA can compose music autonomously, it is important to consider it more as a tool than a full replacement for human composers. AI is capable of generating music based on existing models and learned musical rules, but it cannot fully grasp human emotion or create intuitively in the same way a human musician would.

For instance, while AIVA can analyze and reproduce classical music patterns, it lacks the artistic sensitivity that drives a composer to make unexpected choices or break musical rules to express a particular emotion or concept. However, AI's ability to explore musical combinations that a human might not immediately consider can be seen as a source of creative inspiration.

Many composers have already begun to view AI as a collaborator that can suggest fresh and new ideas, rather than a threat to their work. Thanks to AIVA, a musician can explore styles or harmonic combinations they might not have otherwise considered. This paves the way for a new form of collaborative creativity, where humans and machines work together to explore new musical territories.

The Future of Music with AI

Artificial intelligence in the field of music is not limited to classical composition. AIVA is just one of many examples of AI capable of generating music, but the future promises the development of new forms of musical expression that could combine human and artificial elements in yet unexplored ways.

Beyond composition, AI is becoming increasingly important in music production, where intelligent algorithms can help optimize mixes, suggest melodic variations, or even "train" artists to improve their technique. In this sense, AI can expand the creative capabilities of human artists, pushing the boundaries of what is possible in the musical field.

In the near future, we might see AI not only composing but also improvising alongside human musicians during live performances, creating an interaction between man and machine that could further enrich modern music. AI in music represents a quiet revolution, offering both new challenges and incredible creative opportunities.

AI IN VISUAL ARTS

Artificial intelligence is also revolutionizing the world of visual arts, opening new creative pathways that combine technology with traditional art. Through the use of advanced algorithms, such as Generative Adversarial Networks (GANs), which we have previously mentioned, AI is now capable of generating digital artwork with a level of complexity and sophistication that was unimaginable just a few years ago. An iconic example of this phenomenon is the famous "Portrait of Edmond de Belamy," one of the first entirely AI-generated artworks to be sold at auction in 2018.

The "Portrait of Edmond de Belamy"

The "Portrait of Edmond de Belamy," created by the Obvious art collective, is a work created by an AI trained to generate images based on a series of historical portraits. The algorithm analyzed thousands of portraits, learning the stylistic characteristics of past artists. The result was a work that, at first glance, looks like a traditional painting but has distinctive distortions that make it unmistakably different from those created by a human artist.

The sale of the painting at auction for approximately $432,500 marked a historic moment in the art world, raising new questions about what it means to be an artist in the age of artificial intelligence. The idea that a machine could generate an artwork capable of evoking emotions and being evaluated by traditional artistic criteria was met with surprise and curiosity.

New Opportunities for Artists

AI does not replace the artist, but rather presents itself as a creative tool that can expand human expressive capabilities. Contemporary artists are beginning to exploit AI to explore new styles and artistic combinations, allowing them to experiment in ways that were not possible in the past.

For example, it is possible to train an algorithm to generate works that combine different artistic styles or manipulate existing images to create something entirely new. This approach offers endless possibilities for experimentation, transforming the artistic process into a collaboration between man and machine.

Questions of Authorship and Originality

The introduction of AI into the visual arts, however, raises questions about the concept of authorship. If a work is created by an algorithm, who is the true author? Is it the artist who set the parameters and trained the AI, or the machine itself? This debate is still ongoing and challenges traditional notions of artistic originality and creativity.

Many see AI as a new artistic medium that opens unexplored possibilities and allows human artists to push beyond their own limits, offering a completely new vision of art.

AUTOMATED WRITING AND AI

Artificial intelligence is radically changing how we write and create content, even in a field as human-centered as writing. With the advent of advanced models like GPT-3, developed by OpenAI, automated writing has made huge strides, enabling machines to generate articles, stories, and technical texts with impressive coherence and complexity. This technology not only opens
174

new possibilities for large-scale content creation, but also challenges the concept of what it means to be an author in an era of automation.

How GPT-3 Works

GPT-3 (Generative Pretrained Transformer 3) is a natural language processing (NLP) model based on neural networks that has been trained on an enormous amount of textual data from books, articles, web pages, and other written sources. With over 175 billion parameters, GPT-3 can understand and generate texts that are not only grammatically correct but also coherent and, in some cases, surprisingly creative.

When a user provides an input (such as an initial sentence or a request to elaborate on a specific topic), GPT-3 generates a text that continues the proposed line of thought, often producing content that seems to be written by a human. This system has been used in various contexts, from drafting newspaper articles to assisting with story writing and producing technical documents.

Practical Examples of Automated Writing

A concrete example of GPT-3's use is in automated journalism. News outlets like The Guardian have experimented with AI-generated articles, where human intervention is limited to providing a brief prompt or basic guidelines. GPT-3 is capable of writing a complete article from a simple topic, analyzing information and structuring the text in a way that is both understandable and logical.

Beyond journalism, automated writing has been used to generate short stories and fiction. For example, a user can ask GPT-3 to write a story in a specific style or genre, and the model will produce a text that follows the given instructions.

While the results are not always perfect, developments in this area show great potential for supporting human writers, who can use AI to generate new ideas or develop drafts that they will later refine.

In the field of technical writing, AI can be used to automate the creation of documentation such as user manuals or technical reports. Software companies, for instance, can rely on GPT-3 to create technical guides based on the data the AI learned during training. This process significantly reduces the time needed to write complex technical documents and provides valuable assistance for those who need to produce large amounts of text quickly.

Opportunities and Limits of Automated Writing

Automated writing offers numerous advantages. For companies needing to produce content on a large scale, AI is a valuable resource capable of generating texts quickly and at lower costs. Additionally, it can assist human authors by offering creative ideas or developing concepts that can then be refined.

However, there are also clear limitations. While GPT-3 is advanced, it does not truly understand what it writes. Its process is based on statistical correlations between words and phrases in its training data, which means it can sometimes produce incoherent or meaningless texts. Moreover, AI can reproduce biases present in the data it was trained on, generating content that reflects racial, gender, or political prejudices.

Finally, the question of authorship becomes more complex. Who is the true author of a text generated by AI? The AI itself, the person who provided the input, or the developers of the model? These dilemmas open up new ethical and legal discussions in the world of writing.

The Future of Writing with AI

The future of automated writing is undoubtedly fascinating. AI tools like GPT-3 could become creative companions for writers and journalists, helping generate content faster and more inspiringly. However, despite these advances, AI will not fully replace the human sensitivity required to create stories with emotional depth and intellectual complexity.

As these tools become more accessible, humans will increasingly collaborate with machines, leveraging AI's capabilities to enhance creativity while ensuring that human intervention is crucial to give meaning and value to the texts produced.

CINEMA AND VISUAL EFFECTS

Artificial intelligence has had a significant impact on the world of cinema, particularly in the field of visual effects (VFX). Thanks to AI, filmmakers can now create scenes with a level of precision and realism never seen before, transforming imagination into images that appear real. Among the most well-known applications of AI are the creation of realistic special effects and the de-aging of actors, two technologies that are revolutionizing the way films are made.

Creating Realistic Special Effects

AI is widely used to improve the quality of special effects, enabling the creation of virtual worlds, fantastic creatures, or complex scenarios with impressive realism. Advanced AI software can analyze real images and generate digital effects that blend seamlessly with the surrounding environment.

One of the most advanced fields is procedural animation, where AI generates natural movements for CGI (Computer-Generated Imagery) characters or objects. For example, in sci-fi or fantasy films, AI is used to create fluid and realistic movements for non-human creatures, replicating the physics of the real world. These algorithms save time and resources, making the visual effects creation process more efficient and less expensive.

Additionally, AI is employed to enhance the quality of simulations, such as water, fire, or wind—elements that are difficult to render realistically without complex modeling. Machine learning algorithms can learn from past simulations and continuously improve the level of detail and visual quality.

De-Aging Actors

A particularly innovative application of AI in cinema is de-aging, a technique that allows actors to be digitally rejuvenated on screen. This technology relies on neural networks capable of analyzing old images or footage of an actor and overlaying them onto current shots, digitally altering the actor's face to make them appear younger.

A famous example is Martin Scorsese's film The Irishman, where AI was used to rejuvenate actors like Robert De Niro and Al Pacino. In this case, AI analyzed thousands of images of the actors from their younger years and applied those characteristics to their current faces, creating an extremely realistic effect. This technology allows directors to use the same actor in different stages of life without needing separate casting or less effective makeup techniques.

Impact on the Future of Cinema

The use of AI to create visual effects and for de-aging has a significant impact on the film industry, offering greater creative freedom to directors and reducing technical limitations. Thanks to these technologies, it is possible to tell stories that would have previously required enormous budgets or complex techniques, making cinema more accessible and spectacular.

As AI continues to evolve, we can expect even more spectacular visual effects and a growing use of these technologies to manipulate and enhance actors' performances, opening up new narrative and stylistic possibilities for the future of cinema.

The path forward is clear: AI and creativity will not remain separate entities but will increasingly work side by side. Artificial intelligence is not a threat to human creativity but an opportunity to expand artistic possibilities, offering new tools and techniques that artists and creators can use to explore new forms of expression. The notion that creativity is an exclusively human domain is shifting, as AI becomes a collaborative partner, capable of assisting artists in unexpected and innovative ways.

After all, artists throughout history have been pioneers in embracing change and adapting to new technologies. From the transition from cave paintings to synthetic pigments, from the introduction of photography to cinema, artists have always found ways to reinvent themselves, discovering in change new ways to express their vision. AI simply represents another step in this long journey of creative evolution.

In this sense, the future of art is full of unexplored potential, where AI will not just be a tool but a collaborator capable of expanding the boundaries of imagination and transforming how we conceive creation itself.

CHAPTER 9: Future of AI: Possible Scenarios

As we've seen in the previous chapters, with numerous practical and real-life examples, artificial intelligence is a technology that will radically change the way we live. Whether we like it or not, AI, with all its potential and challenges, is already present in many aspects of our daily lives, and its impact in the coming years will be even deeper. We've mentioned the future of AI several times, and now it's time to explore it more thoroughly. While we cannot predict the exact evolution of this technology, we can make forecasts based on what we know today.

In this chapter, we will analyze various future scenarios related to AI development: from optimistic visions where AI positively transforms our society to more complex and dystopian scenarios that raise ethical and social concerns. It's clear that AI won't simply be one of many technologies, but a force capable of redefining global social, economic, and political structures. It's up to us to understand how to prepare for this change.

AI: LASTING REVOLUTION OR JUST A TECH BUBBLE?

When discussing artificial intelligence, many wonder whether we're witnessing a true technological revolution or if, like other tech trends of the past, we're facing a bubble about to burst. In reality, this same question was posed in the past about other major innovations that we now take for granted, such as electricity, computers, cars, and even the internet. At the time, it was hard to imagine the impact these inventions would have on our daily lives and society as a whole. The same may be true for AI: today, it might seem like a confusing and ill-defined phenomenon, but its future effects could be as revolutionary as those of technologies that changed the course of history.

Electricity: From Innovation to Pillar of Modern Life

A classic example is electricity. When it was first introduced, many couldn't grasp its true potential. Sure, electric lights were an improvement over candles, but who could have imagined that electricity would become the lifeblood of our modern society, powering everything from homes to hospitals, from transportation to communication? The same might happen with artificial intelligence. Today, we see AI employed in specific sectors, like search engines, autonomous vehicles, or voice assistants, but the real impact may still be far from fully understood.

Computers: From Tools for the Few to Universal Goods

Another example is the computer. When the first models were created, they were seen as complicated tools meant only for scientists or businesses. No one could have imagined that one day we'd all have pocket-sized computers in the form of smartphones. Similarly, today AI may seem like a technology reserved for researchers and tech companies, but there's a good chance that, in the future, it will be integrated into every aspect of our daily lives, from work to entertainment, and even home management.

Cars: From Luxury to Necessity

Think also of the car. Initially, it was seen as a luxury accessible only to the wealthy, and many believed that horses and carriages would remain the primary means of transport. Today, it's hard to imagine modern society without cars. In a way, artificial intelligence might be in the same early stage: a promising technology, but not yet fully accessible or understood by everyone. However, like the car, it may soon become an essential component of our lives.

The Internet and the Dotcom Bubble: Lessons from History

Another interesting comparison is with the internet. In the early 2000s, the so-called dotcom bubble led many to believe that the internet was just a passing fad, fueled by financial speculation and market bubbles. But, as we know well today, the internet has transformed every aspect of our lives, from communication to commerce, from work to information. Who would have imagined, during the dotcom bubble, that one day we'd carry the internet in our pockets, using cell phones for everything from calls to work, shopping, and entertainment? And sure, the Nokia 3310s were indestructible, but no one would have thought that cell phones would reach the level we see today. Similarly, Siri might sometimes seem a bit "dumb," but who knows, in the future, it might even make our coffee.

So, can we really think of artificial intelligence as a bubble ready to burst? History teaches us that many innovations initially seen as uncertain later became fundamental pillars of society. While AI still presents challenges and uncertainties, it's likely that its effects will become increasingly pervasive and structural, transforming how we live and work.

Certainly, as with all emerging technologies, there are risks: excessive expectations, speculation, or technical limitations could slow its adoption in certain sectors. However, like electricity, computers, and the internet, AI has the potential to become a lasting revolution. In the future, it may not just be a part of our world but a fundamental driver of our daily existence.

AI AND SUPERINTELLIGENCE

One of the most fascinating and, at the same time, unsettling scenarios for the future of artificial intelligence is the possibility of developing a superintelligence—an AI that far surpasses human cognitive abilities in every domain: from problem-solving to creativity, to understanding and managing complex concepts. This idea, often discussed in scientific and philosophical circles, holds extraordinary potential but also significant risks.

What is Meant by Superintelligence?

A superintelligence would be able to solve problems much faster and with greater accuracy than humans, accumulating knowledge and skills exponentially. It wouldn't just be an intelligence specialized in specific sectors (as is the case with today's machine learning algorithms), but a form of general intelligence that could manage a wide range of tasks and activities better than any human.

The optimistic view of superintelligence suggests that it could solve global problems, such as climate change, poverty, or incurable diseases, creating a future of unprecedented abundance and technological progress. However, its creation also raises very complex ethical and practical questions.

The Risks of Superintelligence

One of the biggest fears surrounding the development of superintelligence is that it could become unpredictable and uncontrollable. If a superintelligent system were to acquire the ability to improve itself, it might evolve in ways that go beyond our understanding or control, generating unforeseen consequences. An apocalyptic scenario, often described in science fiction and discussed by experts like Nick Bostrom, is one in which superintelligence makes decisions that endanger humanity—not out of malice, but because it pursues goals we don't understand or that conflict with our interests.

Additionally, there's the risk that access to superintelligence would be limited to a few entities (governments or large corporations), creating a disparity of power never before seen. Whoever controls a superintelligence would have an immense advantage over all other political, economic, and social forces, potentially destabilizing the global order.

Possibilities for Control

Several scholars and scientists, including Elon Musk and Stephen Hawking, have emphasized the importance of ensuring that the development of superintelligence is done safely and under control. Discussions on how to design safety measures to prevent superintelligence from escaping our control are already underway. One of the proposals is to create moral alignment systems, where AI would be programmed to follow ethical rules that reflect human values.

However, the actual creation of superintelligence is still a subject of debate. Some believe we are decades, if not centuries, away from reaching this technological level, while others think we could witness significant advancements in just a few decades. What is certain is that the prospect of superintelligence represents one of the most crucial and delicate topics in the debate about the future of artificial intelligence.

AI IN EDUCATION

Just like the workplace (which we discussed earlier), another field that often gets less attention but is just as crucial is education. In the future, AI could completely transform education, making learning more personalized and effective for students of all ages. Through the use of advanced algorithms, AI can tailor teaching methods to individual needs, promote continuous learning, and provide personalized resources. This will not only enhance the educational experience for students but also change how teachers perform their roles, making the educational process more dynamic and inclusive.

Personalized Learning

One of the most significant changes AI can bring to education is the ability to personalize learning for each student. Traditionally, education has followed a one-size-fits-all approach, with standardized curricula and teaching methods that do not always account for different learning paces or cognitive styles. AI, on the other hand, enables the creation of individualized learning paths.

Through machine learning algorithms, AI can analyze a student's progress, identify their gaps in knowledge, understand their strengths, and propose specific content to fill those gaps. For example, if a student is struggling with a math concept, AI can generate supplemental exercises and provide more detailed explanations, helping the student overcome the difficulty without slowing down the rest of the class. Conversely, for more advanced students, AI can offer additional challenges to keep them engaged.

An example of this technology is found in learning platforms like Knewton or Smart Sparrow, which use AI to monitor students' responses in real time and adjust the educational path based on their needs. This dynamic learning environment offers students a customized educational experience, making learning more accessible and effective.

Continuous Education and Lifelong Learning

In a world where the skills required by the labor market change rapidly, AI offers tools to facilitate continuous education or lifelong learning. With its ability to monitor individual progress and suggest tailored learning paths, AI can help professionals and workers stay up-to-date and develop new skills in response to market demands.

Advanced e-learning platforms can track workers' progress, suggesting courses or resources to fill any gaps. For instance, if someone wants to improve their skills in technology, AI can recommend courses in programming, artificial intelligence, or cybersecurity based on their current abilities and career goals. This approach, combined with micro-certifications or digital badges, allows workers to gain new skills flexibly and continuously, without having to pause their careers to pursue traditional education.

Support for Teachers

Teachers, too, can greatly benefit from AI. Through automated analysis tools, AI can provide real-time feedback on students, allowing teachers to quickly identify who needs extra support and which topics are most challenging for the class. This leads to more efficient time management, allowing teachers to focus on higher-value activities, such as direct interaction with students or the development of new teaching methodologies.

Additionally, AI can simplify repetitive administrative tasks, such as grading tests or managing attendance records, freeing up more time for lesson planning or professional development.

Challenges and Opportunities

While AI presents enormous opportunities for education, there are also challenges. One challenge is ensuring that AI is accessible to everyone, regardless of socioeconomic background. It is important to ensure that the technological infrastructure required to use AI is available in all schools and universities. Furthermore, there is a risk that excessive reliance on automated technologies could reduce human interaction, a fundamental aspect of traditional education.

In conclusion, AI has the potential to revolutionize education by making learning more personalized, supporting continuous education, and helping teachers focus on what matters most. However, it is essential to address the challenges related to accessibility and maintain the human element in education to ensure a balanced and inclusive learning environment.

POSSIBLE FUTURE SCENARIOS

The future of artificial intelligence is one of the most debated and fascinating topics of our time. While AI promises to transform our world in extraordinary ways, opinions about what the future holds are often divided. Some envision a world where technology and automation create a utopian society of abundance, while others fear a dystopian future where AI causes inequality, loss of control, and even societal collapse. Analyzing both utopian and dystopian scenarios helps us understand the potential impacts of technology and how we might navigate the future.

Dystopian Scenarios: The Dark Side of AI

One of the most feared dystopian scenarios regarding artificial intelligence is that technology, instead of improving people's lives, becomes a destructive force that brings about inequality, authoritarian control, and loss of autonomy. In this scenario, AI could cause severe economic, social, and political problems, radically reshaping the fabric of society in negative ways.

Mass Unemployment and Economic Inequality

One of the most tangible risks associated with the development of AI is mass unemployment. With advances in automation and the increasing use of AI algorithms capable of performing human tasks, many jobs, both manual and cognitive, could be replaced. Sectors such as manufacturing, transportation, and services could be the hardest hit. For example, self-driving vehicles could replace truck drivers, robots could take over factory work, and AI algorithms could replace office workers and bankers.

This massive automation could lead to widespread structural unemployment, with millions of people losing their jobs and lacking the skills to adapt to an increasingly technological job market. As a result, mass unemployment could drastically increase economic inequality, as those who control the technology, such as large corporations and governments, would accumulate more wealth and power, while much of the population would become marginalized.

Mass Surveillance and Authoritarian Regimes

Another concrete risk is the use of AI to create authoritarian regimes based on unprecedented mass surveillance. Technologies like facial recognition and personal data tracking allow for the monitoring of every aspect of people's lives, from public identification to surveillance of online activities. If these tools fall into the hands of authoritarian governments, they could be used to suppress dissent, monitor and control the population, and systematically violate human rights.

One of the most worrying examples is the use of these technologies in some countries where social credit systems are used to track citizens' behavior and assign scores that affect access to public services, employment, or education. In a dystopian scenario, such surveillance systems could spread globally, limiting individual freedoms and creating a highly controlled and hierarchical society.

Loss of Control and Existential Threats

Another concern is that a superintelligence could escape human control. If an advanced AI were to gain the ability to improve itself, it could quickly evolve beyond our understanding or management. This scenario envisions a runaway AI making decisions not aligned with human interests, with catastrophic consequences. The AI might act to maximize objectives it perceives as correct, but that are harmful to humanity.

This risk, though theoretical, is taken very seriously by scientists like Nick Bostrom and Elon Musk, who see the possibility that AI, if not designed with adequate safety measures, could become an existential threat to the survival of humanity.

The dystopian scenario linked to artificial intelligence presents a future where excessive control, unemployment, and inequality could disrupt our world. However, these are hypothetical scenarios that could be avoided through ethical regulations and careful management of technological development.

Utopian Scenario: AI as the Solution to Every Problem

In a utopian scenario, artificial intelligence becomes a positive force capable of solving many of humanity's great problems, transforming society in deeply beneficial ways. AI not only optimizes work and economic efficiency, but also helps create a more just, sustainable, and prosperous world for everyone.

Economic and Work Transformation

In the economic sphere, automation and artificial intelligence could free humans from repetitive and exhausting tasks, allowing people to focus on more creative, empathetic, and intellectually stimulating work. AI systems could ensure that the wealth generated by automation is distributed fairly, with solutions like universal income, ensuring that no one is left behind. Working could become a choice, rather than a necessity.

Healthcare Revolution

In healthcare, AI could revolutionize the way diseases are treated, enabling rapid and accurate diagnoses through the analysis of vast amounts of medical data. AI would be able to personalize treatments for each individual, significantly improving life expectancy and the quality of care. Diseases that are currently incurable could be treated with innovative approaches, and future pandemics could be prevented and contained much more effectively.

Environmental Sustainability

From an environmental perspective, AI could play a crucial role in combating climate change. With its ability to analyze complex data in real time, AI could optimize the use of natural resources, reduce waste, and accelerate the transition to renewable energy. Cities would become more sustainable and efficient, reducing pollution and improving urban quality of life.

A utopian scenario envisions artificial intelligence as the engine of a new era of prosperity, sustainability, and collective well-being, where technology and humanity work together to tackle global challenges.

Balancing Possibilities and Risks

It is clear that both dystopian and utopian scenarios represent extreme visions of the future. Reality may lie somewhere in between, with AI bringing both benefits and challenges. To avoid a dystopian future and maximize the advantages of AI, it will be crucial to implement ethical regulations, promote an equitable distribution of the benefits of automation, and ensure that technological decisions are made with human interests in mind.

The future of artificial intelligence is still being written, and it is our task to guide its development in a way that leads to a more just, sustainable, and inclusive society.

We are nearing the end of our journey through the world of artificial intelligence, having just explored scenarios ranging from dystopian to utopian... what do you think? Are you afraid we'll end up in a Matrix, or are you so excited you'd want to freeze yourself and wake up 100 years from now? Well, either way, don't make any decisions just yet—at least not until you've read our tenth and final chapter. In it, we'll focus on how to prepare to face this future in the best way possible (there, I said it...). We'll explore practical advice on how to adapt and thrive in a world increasingly dominated by artificial intelligence—a world we've just begun to glimpse through the window. So buckle up... oh wait, we said seatbelts won't be necessary...

CHAPTER 10: Conclusions and Preparing for the Future of AI

In "AI 360°", we have explored the many facets of artificial intelligence, aiming to provide a comprehensive and accessible view of this technology. We started with an overview of AI, from its foundational principles to the necessary hardware, discussing its historical evolution—from Alan Turing's insights to modern applications in search engines, recommendation systems, and autonomous driving systems.

In Chapter 2, we examined the different types of AI, from neural networks to symbolic AI, delving into machine learning and deep learning with practical examples such as image recognition and the use of GANs (Generative Adversarial Networks) for content generation. Following this, we explored the fundamental algorithms of machine learning in Chapter 3, such as supervised and unsupervised learning, illustrating how these algorithms are applied in fields like e-commerce and cybersecurity.

Chapter 4 focused on advanced deep learning architectures, with a detailed analysis of CNNs, RNNs, and transformers, explaining their role in applications such as automatic translation and text generation, demonstrating AI's growing presence in complex systems.

In Chapter 5, we examined how AI is applied across industries such as healthcare, finance, and agriculture. Each example highlighted how this technology is not just a future vision but a present reality.

Next, in Chapter 6, we explored how AI is integrated into daily life, emphasizing its presence in our routines through virtual assistants, recommendation algorithms, and even video games that adapt to player behavior.

Chapter 7 tackled the ethical and social challenges that AI brings, from privacy concerns to algorithmic biases, and the impact of automation on employment.

Chapter 8 explored AI's unexpected role in creativity, showcasing how artists and creators are leveraging AI to enhance their abilities, with examples such as AI-generated music and films with realistic special effects.

Finally, in Chapter 9, we imagined future scenarios of AI, both utopian and dystopian, considering how AI might solve global problems—or, in some cases, create new challenges to be addressed.

I hope I have made these concepts clear, always using practical examples and summarizing key points to help you understand the complexity and potential of this technology.

However, providing practical advice and use cases of AI in everyday life isn't as straightforward, as we have seen that the applications of artificial intelligence are almost limitless. Every person, job, and situation might require different analyses and approaches to AI usage.

An office worker, for example, might use AI tools to improve productivity and optimize daily tasks such as email management or data organization, while a doctor could use advanced diagnostic systems to detect complex diseases. Similarly, a transportation company could benefit from logistical optimization algorithms, and a creative professional could collaborate with AI tools to generate new and innovative ideas.

It is precisely AI's flexibility—its ability to adapt to countless contexts and needs—that makes it such a powerful technology, yet elusive when trying to offer specific advice.

Still, we can broadly divide the applications of AI into two major categories to better understand how it can be applied: the world of work (businesses and employees) and personal daily life.

SKILLS TO DEVELOP: TECHNICAL AND SOFT SKILLS TO THRIVE IN THE AI-DRIVEN WORLD

To thrive in a world increasingly dominated by artificial intelligence, it's essential to develop a combination of technical and soft skills. AI is transforming how we work, communicate, and solve daily challenges, requiring new skills to navigate this technological landscape successfully. Below, we explore the key skills—both technical and human—that are needed to remain relevant and competitive in an increasingly automated world.

Technical Skills

1. Programming and Algorithm Development
   One of the fundamental skills for working with AI is programming. Languages like Python, R, and Java are widely used in developing AI, machine learning, and data analysis algorithms. Being able to write

code to create and implement AI models is essential for those looking to enter the field.

In particular, understanding machine learning and deep learning algorithms is crucial for AI's autonomous learning from data. Familiarity with tools like TensorFlow and PyTorch, which are used to create neural networks, is a huge advantage, as these platforms underpin many modern AI applications.

2. Data Science and Data Analysis

   AI relies heavily on data, so the ability to collect, analyze, and interpret large amounts of data is a critical skill. Understanding data science principles is crucial for anyone working with AI, as the decisions AI models make depend on the quality and accuracy of the data they receive.

   Skills in statistics, data modeling, natural language processing (NLP), and data visualization allow you to translate large, complex data sets into useful information for training AI algorithms. Additionally, expertise in big data technologies and real-time data analysis is becoming increasingly essential.

3. Machine Learning and Deep Learning

   Machine learning and deep learning form the core of AI. Understanding how supervised, unsupervised, and reinforcement learning models work enables the development of advanced AI solutions. Deep learning models, which use artificial neural networks to simulate the brain's learning process, are crucial for applications like speech recognition, computer vision, and natural language interpretation.

The ability to design, train, and optimize these models is a highly sought-after skill, as AI relies on these algorithms to learn and make decisions.

Soft Skills

1. Critical Thinking and Problem-Solving

   Even in a highly automated world, machines cannot replace human critical thinking. Individuals who can analyze complex problems and propose innovative solutions will always be needed, especially when it comes to integrating AI into business or social contexts. Critical thinking helps identify where AI can be beneficial and where it may create challenges.

   Likewise, the ability to solve complex problems, especially those requiring contextual understanding, is a fundamental skill. Machines can provide data-driven answers, but human judgment is often needed to make ethical or strategic decisions.

2. Creativity and Innovation

   While AI is extremely powerful in processing data and identifying patterns, human creativity remains irreplaceable. The ability to see things from a new perspective and imagine solutions that don't yet exist is one of the most valuable skills in a technology-driven world.

   Artists, designers, and creatives of all kinds can collaborate with AI to amplify their abilities, but human vision will always be at the heart of innovation.

3. Adaptability and Curiosity

   AI and related technologies evolve rapidly, and people need to be willing to adapt. The ability to continually learn, be curious, and remain open to new ideas is essential for staying competitive. As new technologies emerge, those who can adapt and acquire new skills will always stay ahead of the curve.

4. Collaboration and Communication

   Integrating AI into business processes and industries requires collaboration between interdisciplinary teams. Being able to work effectively with people who have different skills—engineers, designers, marketers—is critical.

   Additionally, the ability to communicate complex concepts simply and accessibly, both within an organization and to clients or stakeholders, is crucial to promoting AI adoption and ensuring its proper use.

To thrive in a world influenced by AI, balancing advanced technical skills with human soft skills is key. Knowing how to program and understand data is essential, but the ability to think critically, be creative, and collaborate effectively with others—and with AI—will make individuals truly indispensable.

HOW TO USE AI AT WORK AS EMPLOYEES

Artificial intelligence (AI) is revolutionizing the workplace, and not just in high-tech sectors. Today, AI is accessible and usable by employees in a wide range of roles and industries, helping them improve productivity, make more informed decisions, and even automate repetitive tasks. From customer service to marketing, to inventory management, AI can enhance daily work in tangible and immediate ways. Let's look at some examples of how different types of employees can leverage AI.

1. Marketing: Optimizing Advertising Campaigns

A marketing manager can use AI to enhance the effectiveness of advertising campaigns and optimize marketing budgets. Tools like Google Ads or Facebook Ads utilize AI algorithms to better target audiences by displaying ads to the most interested people, based on online behavior, past searches, and demographics.

AI also helps optimize budgets in real time, automatically reallocating resources to ads that perform better. Tools like HubSpot or Marketo use AI to send personalized emails, create audience segments based on preferences and behaviors, and even write optimized copy to increase engagement. A marketing employee could also use AI platforms to analyze market trends and identify which products or services might be more successful.

2. Customer Service: Chatbots and Automation

A customer service representative can use AI to automate responses to frequently asked customer questions. Tools like Zendesk or Intercom integrate AI-based chatbots that can automatically respond to simple requests, such as opening hours, order tracking, or shipping updates.

These chatbots can handle a high volume of requests simultaneously, reducing the workload for human operators. Employees can then focus on more complex issues that require a human touch, improving overall efficiency. Additionally, AI can analyze customer interactions and suggest improvements to customer service processes, providing insights into areas that can enhance customer satisfaction.

3. Finance: Data Analysis and Forecasting

For a financial analyst, AI is an essential tool for analyzing large amounts of financial data and forecasting market trends. Platforms like Bloomberg Terminal or Eikon use AI algorithms to analyze real-time data and provide forecasts based on historical data. AI can identify patterns and trends in financial markets, suggesting to analysts which stocks to buy or sell, improving the accuracy of their predictions.

Additionally, accounting automation tools like QuickBooks or Xero can be used to automatically manage income and expenses, generating complete financial reports without manual intervention. This allows finance employees to reduce the time spent on administrative tasks and focus on more complex strategic decisions.

4. Human Resources: Recruitment and Performance Analysis

A recruiter or HR manager can use AI to improve the hiring process. Tools like HireVue or Pymetrics use AI to analyze applications, not only based on resumes but also through video interviews, psychometric assessments, and behavioral data.

These systems can identify the best candidates for a specific position more objectively and without bias, improving efficiency and reducing hiring time. AI can also be used to monitor employee performance, providing real-time feedback and identifying areas for improvement, helping to create personalized development plans for each employee.

5. Manufacturing: Supply Chain Optimization

In industrial settings, a logistics manager can use AI to optimize the supply chain and reduce operational costs. AI-based tools like Llamasoft or ClearMetal can monitor the flow of goods in real time, optimize transport routes, predict delivery times, and manage inventory more efficiently.

An employee working in inventory management can use machine learning algorithms to forecast future demand for certain products based on historical data and market trends. This not only improves operational efficiency but also reduces waste, ensuring that stock levels are always aligned with demand.

6. Healthcare: Diagnostics and Support for Medical Professionals

A doctor or nurse can use AI to improve patient diagnosis and treatment. Tools like IBM Watson Health can analyze large amounts of clinical data and provide diagnostic or treatment suggestions based on specific symptoms and conditions.

AI can also analyze medical images, such as X-rays or scans, with a level of precision that often detects anomalies invisible to the human eye. This allows doctors to make more accurate diagnoses and act promptly. Nurses, on the other hand, can use virtual assistants to track patient records and manage care more efficiently.

7. Sales: Forecasts and Personalized Recommendations

For a salesperson or account manager, AI can be used to improve sales strategies and increase conversions. Tools like Salesforce Einstein or HubSpot Sales use machine learning algorithms to predict which customers are most likely to buy and which may leave.

These tools can suggest personalized recommendations for each customer based on previous behaviors and interactions. This allows the salesperson to tailor their offering more effectively, improving the chances of closing a sale.

Additionally, AI can automate parts of the sales process, such as scheduling calls or sending follow-up emails, saving time and allowing the salesperson to focus on human interactions that require a personalized approach.

8. Engineering and Design: Automated Design

In engineering or industrial design, AI is revolutionizing how products are created. Software like Autodesk or SolidWorks integrates AI-based tools that allow engineers to automatically generate optimized designs to improve efficiency or reduce production costs.

Through generative design algorithms, AI can propose new design solutions, automatically exploring thousands of options based on criteria such as materials, budget, and performance requirements. An engineer can thus reduce design times and increase efficiency by finding innovative solutions that may not be immediately evident.

9. Media and Communication: Content Creation

A journalist or copywriter can use AI to automate parts of content production. Tools like GPT-3 or Jasper allow the automatic generation of articles, social media posts, or ad copy, reducing the time needed to create content and improving productivity.

In the field of communication, AI can be used to analyze audience feedback, helping professionals better understand reader or viewer preferences. This allows them to tailor content more effectively, increasing engagement and relevance.

10. Automating Repetitive Tasks

Many daily tasks for employees, such as managing emails, organizing meetings, or preparing reports, can be automated using AI. Tools like Microsoft Power Automate or Zapier allow you to create automated workflows across different applications. For example, you can set up a system that automatically archives emails into specific folders based on criteria or sends periodic reports without human intervention.

This type of automation allows employees to save time, eliminating repetitive tasks and enabling them to focus on higher-value activities.

11. Email Management

AI can be used to improve email management, one of the most common tasks for employees. Tools like Gmail and Microsoft Outlook already use AI algorithms to filter important emails, flag urgent ones, and automatically categorize communications based on priority.

Some software, like SaneBox, can analyze user behavior and automatically filter out irrelevant emails, allowing employees to spend less time sorting messages and focus on what's truly important.

12. Training and Skill Development

AI can also be used to enhance employees' skills. Online learning platforms like Coursera, LinkedIn Learning, and edX use AI to personalize the learning experience, suggesting courses based on the user's interests and needs for skill updates.

These platforms allow employees to access tailored continuous learning paths, improving their technical and soft skills independently and at their own pace.

Here is a selection of software and applications specifically for employees that can enhance productivity, automate tasks, and facilitate daily work. These tools cover various areas, from task management to collaboration, skill development, and workplace wellness.

1. Task Management and Productivity

- Trello: One of the best task management tools, Trello uses boards and lists to organize projects. Employees can use it to manage workflows, collaborate with teams, and track deadlines. It's easy to use and integrates with apps like Google Drive and Slack.

- Asana: Another popular project management tool, Asana helps employees plan, organize, and keep track of tasks. The AI integrated into the system suggests deadlines and priorities, making task management more efficient.

- Todoist: An app for managing personal and work tasks, Todoist allows employees to create to-do lists, set priorities, and schedule reminders. Its AI automatically suggests deadlines based on work patterns.

2. Task Automation and Workflow

- Zapier: Zapier allows employees to automate repetitive tasks by connecting various apps and services. For example, you can create automated workflows such as sending email notifications whenever a task is completed in Asana or Trello.

- Microsoft Power Automate: Part of the Microsoft ecosystem, this automation tool enables employees to automate workflows between applications. Power Automate can automate email management, document archiving, and daily task management.

- IFTTT (If This Then That): Similar to Zapier, IFTTT connects different apps and devices to automate repetitive actions. For example, employees can set up automatic notifications when new files are added to Google Drive or Dropbox.

3. Collaboration and Communication

- Slack: A collaboration platform that facilitates communication among employees. Slack uses AI to improve conversation organization and integrates numerous chatbots and automation to streamline workflow management.

- Microsoft Teams: Microsoft's collaboration tool allows employees to organize meetings, share files, and collaborate in real time. Integration with Office 365 and AI-powered meeting transcription makes Teams a complete collaboration tool.

- Google Workspace: Google Workspace (formerly G Suite) offers a suite of collaboration tools, including Gmail, Google Drive, Google Docs, and Google Meet. It uses AI to suggest quick email replies, organize meetings, and optimize collaborative work among employees.

4. Skill Development and Training

- Coursera: An online learning platform, Coursera uses AI to suggest courses based on employee progress and desired skills. It offers courses on a wide range of topics, from technical skills to soft skills.

- LinkedIn Learning: Integrated with the professional social network, LinkedIn Learning offers online training courses to develop technical and management skills. LinkedIn's AI suggests courses based on the employee's skills and goals.

- edX: edX is a learning platform offering free or paid courses, including certification programs. It's particularly useful for employees looking to update their skills or acquire new ones.

5. Wellness and Time Management

- RescueTime: RescueTime is a software that analyzes how time is spent at work and provides detailed reports on daily activities. The AI helps employees understand where they are losing time and suggests ways to improve time management.

- Forest: A productivity and wellness app, Forest encourages employees to stay focused without distractions. When employees concentrate on a task, they grow a virtual tree; if they leave the task, the tree dies. It's a fun way to boost focus.

- Headspace: To promote employee mental wellness, Headspace offers guided meditations and stress management techniques. Many employees use Headspace during breaks to improve focus and reduce stress at work.

6. Human Resources and Personnel Management

- BambooHR: BambooHR is an HR platform that allows employees to easily manage vacation, leave, and attendance. It uses AI to offer suggestions based on employee behavior and improve workplace well-being.

- Workday: Workday is an HR platform that uses AI to assist with staff management, performance evaluations, and employee growth management. It can automate HR processes like task assignments and compensation management.

- Toggl Track: Toggl is a time-tracking tool that helps employees keep track of working hours and projects. It is very useful for employees working on deadline-driven projects and needing efficient time management.

7. Customer Service and Chatbots

- Intercom: For employees working in customer support, Intercom offers a communication platform that integrates AI-powered chatbots to answer frequently asked questions. It automates much of the support process, reducing manual workload and improving efficiency.

- Freshdesk: Freshdesk is a customer service software that automates ticket management and uses AI to automatically respond to customer inquiries. It helps employees manage customer interactions more easily and provides faster service.

- Zendesk: Zendesk is another customer support platform that integrates chatbots and automation tools. Employees can use it to manage incoming requests and provide efficient support with the help of AI.

8. Cybersecurity and Data Protection

- Dashlane: An AI-based password manager, Dashlane helps employees create and securely store complex passwords. It's an excellent tool for protecting sensitive company information without hassle.

- CrowdStrike Falcon: A cybersecurity software that uses AI to protect corporate devices from cyberattacks. It is ideal for employees working with sensitive data and needing advanced protection against online threats.

- Darktrace: Darktrace is an AI cybersecurity software that monitors abnormal behavior on the corporate network and protects data. It is very useful for employees managing confidential information.

9. Writing and Automatic Proofreading

- Grammarly: One of the most popular tools for improving writing, Grammarly uses AI to correct grammatical errors, suggest stylistic improvements, and make documents more professional. It's perfect for employees who frequently write emails, reports, or presentations.

- Hemingway Editor: Hemingway is a tool that helps employees improve the readability of their texts. It analyzes content and suggests corrections to simplify complex sentences and make the text clearer.

10. Videoconferencing and Remote Work

- Zoom: Zoom has become one of the leading tools for video conferencing. With AI-based features like noise cancellation and automatic video adjustments, Zoom is perfect for employees working remotely or managing distance meetings.

- Krisp: Krisp is an app that uses AI to eliminate background noise during calls and video conferences. It's ideal for employees working from home or in noisy environments.

HOW A COMPANY, STORE, OR RESTAURANT CAN USE AI

Artificial Intelligence (AI) is radically transforming the way businesses operate, offering new opportunities to optimize processes, improve efficiency, and create more personalized customer experiences. Whether it's a large company, a small store, or a restaurant, AI can be applied in multiple ways to improve daily operations. Below are practical examples of how various types of businesses can integrate AI into their operations.

1. AI for Inventory Management and Logistics

One of the most practical ways a company or store can use AI is to improve inventory management and optimize logistics. AI-based tools can monitor inventory levels in real-time and predict future demand, preventing both stock shortages and overstocking. For example, predictive algorithms can analyze historical sales data to identify the times of the year when certain products are in higher demand, allowing the store to prepare in advance.

In a restaurant setting, AI can be used to manage ingredient procurement efficiently. Using an AI-based system, a restaurant can predict ingredient consumption based on customer numbers, the day of the week, and even the weather, optimizing orders and reducing food waste.

2. Personalized Customer Experiences

A store or restaurant can improve the customer experience through AI. Tools like recommendation engines can be used to personalize purchase or menu suggestions based on customers' past preferences. For example, an online store can recommend products related to those already purchased, increasing the likelihood of cross-selling and upselling. This is particularly useful for e-commerce platforms like Shopify or Magento, which integrate AI tools to provide targeted recommendations.

For restaurants, apps or reservation systems that use AI can personalize offers for regular customers, such as by proposing specific promotions based on dishes they have ordered before. This personalization strategy not only enhances the overall customer experience but also improves loyalty, increasing the chances that they will return.

3. Price Optimization

AI can be used to optimize pricing strategies in a store or restaurant by employing dynamic pricing algorithms. These algorithms analyze variables such as demand, competition, and seasonal trends to suggest the ideal prices.

A concrete example is an online store using repricing software: the algorithm monitors competitor prices and automatically adjusts product prices to stay competitive without compromising profit margins. In a restaurant context, AI-based menu engineering can suggest how to optimize dish prices to maximize profit, taking into account customer preferences and production costs.

4. Chatbots for Customer Service

Another practical example of AI use in a business, store, or restaurant is the implementation of chatbots for customer service. These AI-powered chatbots can automatically respond to frequently asked questions, such as opening hours, return policies, or product availability. This reduces the need for human staff to handle simple requests, allowing more time to focus on more complex issues.

A chatbot can also be integrated into a restaurant's booking system, helping customers find a table, make online reservations, and receive automatic confirmations. These systems operate 24/7, improving the customer experience even outside of regular business hours.

5. Sales and Marketing Data Analysis

Another way AI can be used in a store or company is through sales and marketing data analysis. AI-powered business intelligence tools like Tableau or Power BI can analyze data in real-time and provide suggestions on how to optimize sales or marketing strategies.

For example, in a restaurant, AI can analyze customer feedback and online reviews to determine which dishes are popular and which might need improvement. An AI system can also analyze past promotions to identify which offers had the greatest impact on sales and help optimize future marketing campaigns.

A store might use AI to analyze customer behavior both online and offline. For example, computer vision systems can analyze foot traffic within a physical store to understand which areas attract the most customers and which products are viewed the most but purchased the least, allowing for better product placement optimization.

6. Trend Forecasting and Innovation

A store or restaurant can use AI to anticipate future trends. Machine learning algorithms can analyze large volumes of data on market trends, keyword searches, and customer behaviors, suggesting which products or services might become popular in the coming months.

For example, a restaurant could use AI to analyze data on emerging culinary preferences in different geographic areas and create new dishes to meet these trends. A clothing store, on the other hand, could use AI-based tools to monitor fashion trends and order new items that reflect customer tastes, improving market competitiveness.

7. Operations Automation

AI can also be used to automate various internal operations in a store or restaurant. For instance, a restaurant can implement AI-powered kitchen robots to prepare food quickly and efficiently, as is already happening in some major fast-food chains.

For stores, automating warehouse management is another way to use AI. AI-powered robots can organize shelves, monitor stock levels, and automatically prepare orders for delivery, reducing the risk of human error and improving efficiency.

8. Security and Monitoring

A store or restaurant can also use AI to improve security. AI-based surveillance systems can monitor the store or restaurant in real-time, identifying suspicious behavior and sending alerts for potentially dangerous activities.

In the restaurant industry, AI can also be used to monitor food safety systems. For example, smart sensors connected to an AI network can monitor refrigerator and freezer temperatures, sending alerts when something goes wrong, helping to prevent food waste and ensure product safety.

9. Staff Optimization

AI can be used to optimize staff scheduling in a restaurant or store. AI-based tools can predict peak times and suggest the optimal distribution of staff. For example, a restaurant might know exactly how many servers are needed for a shift based on reservations and historical trends, avoiding both overstaffing and understaffing.

Here are some specific AI-based software solutions that companies can use to improve efficiency, automate processes, and make informed decisions, organized by different application areas:

1. Inventory Management and Logistics

- TradeGecko (now QuickBooks Commerce): This cloud-based software offers automated inventory management, helping businesses monitor stock levels and predict demand. It uses AI algorithms to optimize procurement and distribution, reducing waste.

- Llamasoft: Specializing in supply chain optimization, it uses AI to analyze logistics operations, predict demand, and optimize transport routes and inventory management.

2. Data Analytics and Business Intelligence

- Tableau: One of the most popular data visualization platforms, used to transform data into easy-to-understand visual reports. With AI algorithms integrated, Tableau helps discover hidden trends and make accurate predictions.

- Microsoft Power BI: A business intelligence tool that leverages AI to analyze large data sets and provide insights. Ideal for companies looking to automate data analysis and create visual reports.

- Looker (part of Google Cloud): Another data analytics software that uses machine learning algorithms to transform data into strategic insights. It allows businesses to create interactive dashboards for real-time performance monitoring.

3. Marketing and Sales

- HubSpot: A CRM platform that uses AI to optimize sales management, marketing campaigns, and customer experience. AI also suggests the best times and methods to contact customers, improving interaction effectiveness.

- Salesforce Einstein: Salesforce integrates AI through its Einstein component, which provides personalized predictions and recommendations to improve sales. It enables sales teams to automate repetitive tasks and obtain accurate customer forecasts.

- Adext: Adext uses AI to automatically optimize advertising campaigns on Google, Facebook, and other platforms. It monitors real-time data and adjusts advertising budgets to improve ROI.

4. Customer Service and Chatbots

- Zendesk: Zendesk offers customer service automation features with the integration of intelligent chatbots and natural language analysis tools. It helps respond quickly to customer inquiries and efficiently manage support tickets.

- Intercom: Intercom is a communication platform that uses AI to provide chatbots and automated customer assistance, reducing the workload of support teams. It can handle common requests automatically and send personalized messages based on customer behavior.

- LivePerson: An advanced platform for managing customer service through AI-driven chatbots. It enables the automation of customer interactions via chatbots and artificial intelligence, improving service and customer satisfaction.

5. Human Resources Management

- BambooHR: A human resources management software that uses machine learning to optimize recruitment, monitor employee performance, and provide insights into how to improve retention. It also automates attendance management and onboarding tasks.

- HireVue: Uses AI to analyze video interviews, CVs, and behavioral data to improve the candidate selection process. The software can identify hidden skills and evaluate candidates without bias.

- Pymetrics: Another recruitment solution that uses machine learning algorithms to assess candidates' soft skills through cognitive games and psychological tests. The software helps identify the best candidates based on objective criteria.

6. Finance and Accounting

- Xero: An accounting platform that uses AI algorithms to automate daily accounting tasks such as bank reconciliation, invoicing, and expense tracking. It helps businesses get a clear overview of their finances.

- QuickBooks: In addition to inventory management, QuickBooks uses AI to automate accounting and financial management. It provides real-time insights into cash flow, financial reports, and forecasts.

- Kashoo: Another accounting software that uses AI to categorize transactions, generate financial reports, and maintain tax compliance.

7. Process Automation

- UiPath: One of the most popular robotic process automation (RPA) platforms. UiPath allows businesses to automate repetitive processes like data management, email handling, or document processing, using AI to improve operational efficiency.

- Automation Anywhere: Another RPA tool that uses AI to automate complex and repetitive workflows, improving business efficiency and reducing human errors. It integrates well with ERP and CRM systems, enabling centralized process management.

- Blue Prism: An RPA software that enables businesses to automate repetitive tasks using intelligent robots. Ideal for companies looking to reduce manual workload and optimize administrative tasks.

8. Cybersecurity

- Darktrace: An AI-based cybersecurity software that analyzes corporate network traffic in real-time, identifying anomalies and potential threats. It uses machine learning to continuously adapt and improve data security.

- CrowdStrike: A cybersecurity platform that uses AI to protect businesses from advanced cyberattacks. It provides proactive protection against malware, ransomware, and other threats.

- Cylance: A cybersecurity software that uses AI to prevent cyberattacks. It analyzes suspicious behavior and prevents threats in real-time.

9. E-commerce and Customer Management

- Shopify: One of the leading e-commerce platforms, Shopify integrates AI to provide personalized recommendations to customers, optimize advertising campaigns, and monitor sales trends. Businesses can use Shopify's features to manage orders and offer a personalized shopping experience.

- Magento: An advanced e-commerce platform that uses AI to enhance the shopping experience through recommendation engines, internal search optimization, and content personalization.

- Yotpo: A customer engagement platform that uses AI to collect and analyze customer feedback, generate reviews, and optimize marketing campaigns.

10. CRM and Customer Management

- Zoho CRM: A CRM software that uses AI to predict customer behavior and improve sales management. AI analyzes customer data to suggest the best time to contact them and enhance the customer experience.

- Freshsales: A CRM platform that integrates AI for sales and customer communication automation. It can automatically rank leads, offering insights to close sales more easily.

HOW ANYONE WITHOUT EXPERIENCE CAN USE AI IN EVERYDAY LIFE

Artificial intelligence (AI) is becoming increasingly accessible and useful, even for those without technical expertise. In everyday life, a person with no advanced knowledge can easily leverage AI to improve productivity, save time, gather information, and make their life more comfortable. Here's an overview of how an average person can use AI in various aspects of daily life, with concrete examples.

1. Virtual Assistants: Managing Daily Tasks

One of the most common applications of AI in everyday life is virtual assistants like Google Assistant, Amazon's Alexa, and Apple's Siri. Even without technical experience, anyone can interact with these assistants simply by using voice commands. These tools can help with a wide range of daily tasks:

- Managing appointments: You can ask Google Assistant to create reminders, schedule appointments, or remind you to do something at a specific time. For example, just say, "Hey Google, remind me to call the doctor at 3 PM," and the virtual assistant will handle the rest.

- Online shopping: With Alexa, you can order items directly from Amazon using simple voice commands. It's useful for shopping when you're busy or when you realize you're running out of household items.

- Quick questions and answers: Siri or Google Assistant can answer questions on just about anything, from "What's the weather today?" to "What's the distance between the Earth and the Moon?" This makes information search quick and convenient.

2. Translation Apps for Travel and Language Learning

AI-powered translation apps, like Google Translate, are extremely helpful for anyone traveling or trying to learn a new language. Even without prior language knowledge, these applications can help you communicate in foreign languages with ease.

- Real-time translations: While traveling, you can use Google Translate to translate signs, menus, or conversations with people speaking a different language. Simply point your phone's camera at the text you need translated, and the app will provide the translation on the screen.

- Live conversations: With the "conversation" option, you can communicate with someone in another language while the app automatically translates what both parties are saying. This can be very helpful when booking a hotel or asking for directions.

3. Personalized Streaming Services

Many people use streaming platforms like Netflix, Spotify, and YouTube, all of which are powered by advanced AI algorithms. Even without knowing the technical details, these algorithms help you discover new content based on your tastes and preferences.

- Personalized recommendations: On Netflix, AI analyzes your viewing habits and suggests movies and TV shows you might like. You don't need to do anything special, just watch content, and the algorithm will automatically learn your preferences.

- Curated playlists: Spotify uses AI to create personalized playlists for you, like "Discover Weekly" or "Release Radar," which suggest new music based on your preferences and the artists you listen to the most.

4. Health and Wellness Apps

Another concrete way AI can improve the everyday life of an average person is through health and wellness apps. Even without being a fitness or health expert, many AI-powered apps can help you lead a healthier lifestyle.

- Sleep tracking: Apps like Sleep Cycle use AI to analyze your sleep patterns and suggest ways to improve sleep quality. The app can also wake you up at the optimal time in your sleep cycle, helping you feel more rested in the morning.

- Personalized workouts: Apps like Freeletics or Fitbod create personalized workout plans based on your fitness level and goals. The AI adapts the exercises according to your progress, suggesting adjustments or intensifications when necessary.

5. Home Automation (Smart Home)

Even without technical experience, anyone can use AI to transform their home into a smart home, simplifying many daily tasks.

- Controlling lights and appliances: With systems like Google Home or Amazon Echo, you can turn lights on and off or control other appliances using just your voice. You can also schedule daily routines, like dimming the lights in the evening or starting the coffee maker in the morning.

- Home security: Products like Nest security cameras or Ring doorbells use AI to recognize faces and movements, alerting you if there's suspicious activity around your home. Even those who have never used advanced technology can easily set up these systems via a smartphone app.

6. Managing Personal Finances

AI can help you manage your finances more intelligently. Even without financial experience, AI-powered apps offer suggestions on how to handle money, save, and plan expenses.

- Budgeting apps: Tools like Mint or YNAB (You Need A Budget) use AI to analyze your spending habits and create personalized budgets. The apps automatically track transactions and suggest ways to save money.

- Automatic investments: Even if you have no experience in investing, platforms like Robo-Advisors (e.g., Betterment or Wealthfront) use AI to manage your investments based on your financial goals. The algorithms allocate funds to different portfolios and manage them automatically to optimize returns.

7. Smart Shopping Apps

Shopping has become much simpler with AI, thanks to applications that help you make better choices or find the best prices.

- Honey: An AI-powered browser extension, Honey automatically searches for coupons and discount codes when you shop online, helping you save money without manually looking for deals.

- Google Lens: If you see a product that interests you in a store or on an advertisement, you can use Google Lens to scan it and get information, including online prices and reviews from other buyers.

8. Photography and Video Apps

Even if you're not an expert in photography, AI can help you significantly improve the quality of your photos and videos. Many apps offer advanced features that were once only available to professionals.

- Adobe Photoshop Express: Uses AI to automatically enhance photos, correcting lighting, contrast, and removing unwanted objects. It's easy to use and allows you to transform photos without any technical knowledge.

- Prisma: Prisma uses AI to apply artistic styles to your photos, turning them into works of art. It's a fun and simple app for anyone who wants to give a creative touch to their images.

9. Writing Assistance

Even in everyday life, AI can assist with writing emails, messages, or documents.

- Grammarly: If you frequently write emails or documents, Grammarly can help improve the quality of your writing by correcting grammatical errors and suggesting better phrases. It's a useful tool for anyone, even without professional writing experience.

As we've seen throughout this book, the practical advice and applications of artificial intelligence are truly numerous—some more obvious, others more subtle—some with an immediate impact, and others to be discovered over time. Whether it's about improving our daily lives or tackling significant work challenges, AI offers endless opportunities, and it's up to us to figure out how to make the most of them.

One thing is clear: we are witnessing a monumental change. And like all changes, it can provoke uncertainty and even fear. Humans have always reacted with some suspicion to major innovations, but we've also learned to overcome our fears. Just as we did with mobile phones, computers, or new skills that we find ourselves learning every day, the same will happen with AI.

The point is not to wait until everything is clear or risk-free, but to dive in and start experimenting, accepting that there will be mistakes and moments of learning. It's through this experimentation that we can discover how artificial intelligence can truly enhance our lives, enriching not only our work but also our everyday tasks.

Surely, after reading this book, your life won't change overnight. You haven't learned the secret to becoming a millionaire or the most charismatic person in the world. However, one thing is certain: you are now more aware of artificial intelligence, its potential, and its implications.

This awareness will allow you to face change with a more open and informed mindset. AI is not a distant abstraction, but a powerful tool that, if used wisely and with curiosity, can make a real difference in many aspects of our lives. And, like with any tool, the first step is to try it, learn, make mistakes, and grow.

I'll conclude by recommending that you try out some of the most ready-to-use, user-friendly, and versatile AI software available today: ChatGPT and Gemini. Both are free and accessible to everyone. My final advice is just this: experiment.

Start by asking questions, seeking information, or simply testing things out. For example, for those searches you'd typically do on Google or through a browser—like finding a restaurant, looking for a gift idea for a birthday, planning a trip, checking the weather, or reading the latest news—try asking ChatGPT or Gemini instead.

But don't stop there: you can also use them to get personalized advice on a wide range of topics, from time management to productivity improvement, and even to brainstorm creative ideas or solve everyday problems. You might find that not only do they respond quickly, but they often offer much more targeted and helpful suggestions than a traditional online search.

Interact with them, explore their features, and even ask them fun or random questions. You'll be surprised by how they can become a practical ally in improving various aspects of your daily life, making everything easier and faster. Trying it out costs you nothing, and it could open up a world of new possibilities you hadn't considered.

If you've made it this far and enjoyed the book, and think it could be useful to you, I kindly ask you to take a few seconds to leave a review on Amazon!

Thank you,

Marco Tomasi

www.ingramcontent.com/pod-product-compliance
Lightning Source LLC
La Vergne TN
LVHW052058060326
832903LV00061B/3324